H18

£3.00

JESUS
AND HIS CONTEMPORARIES

JESUS

AND HIS CONTEMPORARIES

Etienne Trocmé

SCM PRESS LTD

Translated by R. A. Wilson from the French
Jésus de Nazareth vu par les témoins de sa vie
published 1972 by Delachaux et Niestlé,
Neuchâtel, Switzerland

334 00767 4

First British edition 1973
published by SCM Press Ltd
56 Bloomsbury Street London

© SCM Press Ltd 1973

Printed in Great Britain by
Cox & Wyman Ltd
London, Reading and Fakenham

To the President and Fellows of
University College, Cambridge,
who by accepting me as one of them in the Spring of 1971
made the writing of this book possible

CONTENTS

INTRODUCTION

There are plenty of books which reveal to their readers the secret of Jesus or offer them the definitive interpretation of one about whom so much has already been written. There are books of this kind to suit every taste, the most simple and the most warped, the most conventional and the most enthusiastic for novelty.

This proliferation and this extreme variety would be no more than natural if they simply reflected an interest in Jesus on the part of all kinds of groups and people. But truth is what every author claims to be expressing, and nearly always tries to impose upon his readers, sometimes with great passion!

Truth is difficult to get at. Historical truth is even more elusive than the related truths which are sought by experiment or reasoning. This is so above all when we are concerned with a person from the distant past who has left no written records. And this is the case with Jesus.

Most of those who set out to enlighten their contemporaries about the prophet of Nazareth have not the slightest idea of the technical complexity of the preliminary studies which they ought to undertake before ever setting pen to paper. As for those who have undertaken this task of documentation and criticism with the seriousness which it requires, they are rarely brave enough to admit to themselves that the results that they have achieved are so complex that their final synthesis includes a good deal of arbitrary simplification.

In the pages that follow I shall try to show that the texts which give us our knowledge of Jesus are much more diverse and much more difficult to analyse than is generally supposed. I shall also do my best to point out how and why they do not lend themselves to a satisfactory synthesis which can be said to be *the* truth about Jesus.

Even if one takes no account of all the opinions of Jesus expressed after his death, and even if one ignores the point of view of contemporaries who remained hostile or indifferent to him, it is possible to reconstruct, from texts which go back to well-disposed witnesses of the life of Jesus, four or five different pictures of this mysterious personality.

Having shown this, we shall have to go on to ask where such a statement, so dismaying to those who are fond of simple truths, can lead. I hope to demonstrate that it does not result in the evaporation of the figure of Jesus Christ, but that on the contrary it represents an appeal to believers to deepen their faith, and an invitation to non-believers not to dodge the problem with which Jesus faces them.

The work that follows is an expansion of the Speaker's Lectures which I gave in 1965–66 at the University of Oxford. My colleagues M. A. Chevallier, President of the Université des Sciences Humaines at Strasbourg, and B. Jay, then Lecturer in the Faculty of Protestant Theology at the same university, were kind enough to read and criticize the manuscript. I thank them for all their suggestions, which were valuable even when I had to reject them.

1

The 'Life of Jesus' Marks Time

As a literary genre, the biography of Jesus is not yet two hundred years old, for the work which is generally regarded as the first, that of H. S. Reimarus, *Von dem Zwecke Jesu und seiner Jünger*, was not published until 1778.[1] That is, it is a relatively new approach, especially since several decades were required for it to reach maturity, so little prepared was the cultural environment to receive it.

The publication in 1835 of *Das Leben Jesu*, by David Friedrich Strauss,[2] and then of the *Vie de Jésus* by Ernest Renan in 1863,[3] represented the full flowering of the biography of Jesus. These were two brilliant works, much more soundly based than those which had preceded them. The conflict which they provoked was so lively that the scientific study of the life of Jesus was stimulated by it, and numerous circles which had hitherto been indifferent began to take an interest in it.

Strauss put forward the idea that the gospel narratives should be understood as above all the symbolic expression of religious ideas, that is, as myths. Thus the principal object of research about Jesus was to distinguish the great theological themes which he illustrated, and a knowledge of the historical reality of the figure of Jesus was of little importance.

Renan gave a narrative of the life of Jesus which was both coherent and attractive, and with a sound scholarly basis. It rejected any theological interpretation in favour of a pscyhological reconstruction of the central person in the drama. The reader was encouraged to accept what he was offered as the normal conclusion of an attentive study of the sources.

Both writers gave rise to a school of followers, in spite of all the controversies which their works provided. Right down to the present day, virtually every biography of Jesus falls into one category or the other, in spite of all the tumult which sometimes conceals the continuity of both. Thus the devastating *Geschichte der Leben-Jesu-Forschung* by Albert Schweitzer[4] did not bring to an end the series of biographies on the lines of Renan, while after 1919 the spectacular return to the type inaugurated by Strauss, on the part of K. L. Schmidt, Rudolf Bultmann and all the other young Turks of 'dialectical theology', did little to modify this. In spite of the unquestioned progress achieved over a century, virtually all the biographies of Jesus which are published at the present day still fall into one or the other of these two basic types.

I

Within the tradition founded by Renan, there are, of course, considerable variations. But the gospels are still regarded as above all accounts of historical facts from which criticism can construct a biography of Jesus, provided all the necessary precautions are taken.

(*a*) A first group believes it possible to fit all the data provided by our sources into the framework of an explanatory theory, usually quite bold, of the person and work of Jesus. We shall ignore romances based on the madness of Jesus or on fanciful psycho-analytical interpretations, and we shall also ignore the recent arguments about homosexuality, in which some people have sought the key to the personality of Jesus. These are curious testimonies to our own age and to the attraction which the prophet of Nazareth still exercises upon many of our contemporaries.

Nor shall we pay much attention to the veritable detective stories which, since the time of Reimarus, some people have persisted in constructing round the crucifixion and resurrection of Jesus. The most recent example of these is a disappointing work by H. Schonfield, *The Passover Plot*.[5] The inadequacy of our sources is not sufficient reason for transforming Jesus and his disciples into characters from Conan Doyle or Agatha Christie.

On the other hand, there is much of interest in certain studies which, though excessively systematic, nonetheless emphasize one aspect of the activity of Jesus to which our documents unquestionably bear witness. Thus when Albert Schweitzer,[6] followed by his disciples, reduced Jesus to the rank of a prophet of the imminent arrival of the end, he made use of a very important aspect of his preaching. He was wrong only in treating this as the principal motivation of his hero when, according to our texts, it is only one aspect of his message.

Similarly, when André Trocmé tones down the thoroughly Marxist theses of Kautsky and Barbusse, and attempts to understand Jesus as a social revolutionary using the word as his only weapon for redistributing riches in Israel,[7] the evidence, based on Luke 4.16ff., may seem rather frail. Nevertheless, it draws attention to a feature which is striking enough in a number of sayings of Jesus about riches: their concern for the poor, but also for the rich, whom the Master sought to liberate.

The attempt is sometimes made, on rather similar lines, to see in Jesus a Jewish nationalist leader, close to the Zealot sect which was committed to the defence of the honour of God by direct action, even to the point of assassination. The basic work is still that of Robert Eisler.[8] But this scholar's ideas have been publicized by an American journalist, Joel Carmichael,[9] and by an English scholar, S. G. F. Brandon.[10] This hypothesis draws attention to the contacts which Jesus certainly had with the Zealots. As Oscar Cullmann has shown quite recently,[11] it becomes absurd the moment one tries to make it the explanatory principle for Jesus' whole career.

Another attempt which is too one-sided is that of Ethelbert Stauffer to make Jesus a representative of radical opposition to Qumran and its ethics.[12] There are indications that Jesus conducted a polemic against the moral ideas of the Essene community. W. D. Davies has made this admirably clear in his great work on the Sermon on the Mount,[13] but it is impossible to reduce everything in the ministry of Jesus to a confrontation of this kind, when one remembers that the gospels have not preserved the least mention of the Essenes and that the prophet of Nazareth was a victim of the same priestly circles as the Teacher of Righteousness before him.

(b) By contrast to the bold theorists who believe that they can explain everything at a single blow, there are other biographers

3

of Jesus who are traditionalists concerned above all to defend the historical truth of the whole gospel, and, in the case of many of them, to defend classical christological doctrine. This means in general that there is a very marked apologetic tendency in their works, and that they run the risk of avoiding numerous problems, such as the disagreements between the gospels and passages as difficult as the infancy narratives of Matthew and Luke.

But serious progress has been made by this school since the time of the works written to refute Renan. These writers make particular use of the increasingly accurate knowledge which we are acquiring every year of the Palestinian background to the life of Jesus. The rabbinic texts, which it is now possible to sift in order to retain only what concerns the first century; the Qumran texts, the study of which has made considerable progress, though it remains unfinished; numerous other archaeological discoveries, which have been particularly numerous since 1945 – all these sources allow us to supplement the meagre data given in the gospels and to paint a very lively background against which a biography of Jesus looks much more convincing. After Dalman, Joachim Jeremias, in his *Jerusalem zur Zeit Jesu*,[14] has given a good example of what can be done in this field, while Robert Aron, in his *Années obscures de Jésus*,[15] has used as biographical data for the life of Jesus many elements from rabbinic sources which describe the family and business life of the time.

But this is only to set the stage. The drama has yet to be written, and this is where the difficulty begins. What is the use of a fine setting, if all one has to put on it is an uncritical paraphrase of the gospel texts? Not only are these documents difficult for modern man to accept as they stand, because of their naïve cosmology, demonology and eschatology, but there are also serious contradictions between them, if only in the chronology and topography of the narrative. Their vagueness is often disconcerting to the historian. In many places they show signs of having been touched up, sometimes drastically. Which is the primitive text of the Beatitudes, Matthew 5 or Luke 6? Or of the Lord's Prayer, Matthew 6 or Luke 11? Or of the words spoken by Jesus at the last meal he took with his disciples, Mark 14, Luke 22 or I Cor. 11?

4

These difficulties do not seem to trouble the traditionalists, who avoid them more or less skilfully. Three examples are sufficient to show this. The historian Daniel-Rops wrote *Jésus en son temps*,[16] which was a perfect example on the one hand of the easy fluency of the thoroughly well-informed professional, and on the other of the refusal of all serious criticism of the gospels, which he seeks simply to harmonize. Annie Jaubert, a first-class specialist in the Judaism of the period between the testaments and in the early history of Christianity, could conclude a remarkable book on the date of the Last Supper with an astonishingly naïve account of the course of the passion of Christ.[17] In these pages she manages to harmonize in every detail the four gospel narratives, between which everyone else agrees that there are serious differences. As for Cardinal Jean Daniélou, a scholar of bold views and unparalleled erudition, in a recent short work he did not hesitate to defend the historicity of the infancy narratives of Matthew and Luke almost in their entirety,[18] in spite of the fact that the profound differences between the two, their isolation within the New Testament and the strongly legendary character of most of what they tell calls for extra critical vigilance on the part of the historian.

No doubt such excesses counterbalance the arbitrary constructions of certain of those who deny the historical existence of Jesus and of the one-sided biographies already mentioned. They are no less regrettable, to the extent that they cause the public to believe that the only choice that has to be made is between extremists and traditionalists. This immediately gives an emotional character to the debate which ought to begin with an intensive study of the documents. Fortunately, this patient work has not been abandoned by scholars who follow the way opened by Renan.

(c) What may be described as the scholarly biography of Jesus is in fact still very much alive, in spite of the attacks upon it by the advocates of dialectical theology between the two world wars. Highly-skilled historians, refusing to be tied by any philosophical system, have gone on patiently gathering the slightest indications concerning the person and work of Jesus of Nazareth, criticizing it on the basis of classical methods and publishing works which sacrifice nothing to the desire for sensation, but present an intellectually satisfying portrait of their subject.

One of the weaknesses of this school, which moreover contains many variations, is that it aims at the production of a full academic biography of Jesus, including as complete a topographical and chronological framework as possible, a psychological interpretation of the central figure and his development, as clear a sociological and legal explanation as possible of the success and subsequent failure and condemnation of its hero, an analysis of the influences to which he was subject and his real originality, etc. This is asking too much of the texts which provide our information.

We shall return to this point with regard to the Christian documents, that is, in the main, the canonical gospels. Let us merely note that the celebrated work by Karl Ludwig Schmidt, *Die Rahmen der Geschichte Jesu*,[19] in which the artificial character of the topographical and chronological outline of the gospels was finally demonstrated, has never been refuted. All too often, its conclusions are simply ignored. As for the non-Christian documents, they are so few and so scanty that all one can hope to find in them is a confirmation of particular points already given in the Christian sources. In fact this group of biographers is obliged rather rapidly to gloss over the inadequacies of their documentation and to build certain of their constructions on fragile foundations.

My purpose in saying this is not merely to denounce the inadequate criticism practised by the more conservative among these biographies, such as that of Vincent Taylor,[20] who is too interested in demonstrating that Jesus had a highly developed 'messianic consciousness', or that of David Flusser,[21] where the historical use made of the gospel narratives of the passion is surprisingly naïve. I would also dispute the way in which many specialists handle the criticism of authenticity or historicity when they study the words or actions of Jesus recounted in the gospels. To dismiss as inauthentic or Hellenistic all the sayings in which Jesus attributes to himself a supernatural role or a more or less messianic title is an all too common error of method which is astonishing to anyone familiar with the Jewish literature of the period between the Testaments, beginning with certain texts from Qumran. To accept as authentic only

6

sayings which contradict the faith of the later church is a sound position only if it is adopted very prudently, for we have a very imperfect knowledge of the faith in question. If such a criterion is applied, there is a risk of having nothing left but a minute residue which simply has to be re-embroidered. This danger is not always avoided by Goguel in his book *La Vie de Jésus*.[22] Norman Perrin has succeeded little better.[23]

Be this as it may, these scholarly biographies of the classical type continue to appear with impressive frequency. Apart from the names already given we should also mention those of Charles Guignebert,[24] Martin Dibelius,[25] Morton S. Enslin,[26] Hans-Werner Bartsch,[27] and C. H. Dodd,[28] to which many others could be added. Even if one considers this kind of biography somewhat old-fashioned, one must recognize that it is still very much alive.

This vitality is shown by a degree of progress which may be slow, but cannot be disputed. Thus what used to be the classic distinction between 'Palestinian' and 'Hellenistic' now receives the necessary degree of modification required by the Qumran discoveries, which have revealed to us a Palestinian Judaism that is much more speculative and much more penetrated by outside influences than the rabbinic literature had hitherto led one to suspect. Similarly, the increasing recognition of the social and political dimensions of the activity of Jesus must be welcomed as a victory for historical good sense over the exaggerated theses of those who completely exclude it and those who regard it as the centre of everything. In this respect, the way has been opened by the works of Oscar Cullmann,[29] while H. W. Bartsch has recently added a number of interesting new suggestions.

Might it be added that these scholarly biographies are the best antidote to the picturesque fantasies of those who deny the historical existence of Jesus? It is enough to compare the conscientious work and the differing but always balanced conclusions of the historians whom we have mentioned with the contortions, allegedly based on a study of comparative religions, and the cavalier attitude to the texts which are characteristic of the 'Jesus-myth' writers, to see which should be taken seriously. A comparison between both schools as to creative fancy would lead to the same conclusion, as will be seen presently.

II

The second line followed by those who are fascinated by the figure of Jesus is that which goes back to D. F. Strauss. It regards our principal documents, the gospels, as sources which give access above all to religious ideas, the narrative having essentially a symbolic or 'mythical' value. According to this approach, the principal task of criticism is to reconstruct the religious message which the authors of these books wished to convey when they spoke of Jesus. According to others, a secondary aim of the study of the gospels is to uncover the historic message of Jesus by extracting it from the mass of later ideas in which it is buried.

(a) For some writers in this group, a mythical interpretation of the gospels ought logically to result in the conclusion which D. F. Strauss did not draw from his study: that Jesus is no more than a mythological figure, to which the evangelists gave historical form at a relatively late date. The idea is not a new one, for Volney wrote as early as 1791 that Jesus was no more than the sun god. But it was not treated at length until the beginning of the twentieth century, since when its advocates have presented it under many different forms. When Holland, Germany and Britain had grown weary of these arguments, they were taken up in France by Paul-Louis Couchoud, from 1923, and Prosper Alfaric, from 1927, to mention only the most important writers. At the same period, Soviet history was flogging the same horse in its ponderous fashion.

The brilliant arguments of Couchoud were easily refuted by Maurice Goguel[30] and then by Alfred Loisy.[31] They face two insurmountable difficulties: first, the absence of all denial of the historical existence of Jesus in antiquity, even amongst the adversaries of Christianity and the heretics who were most inclined to deny the humanity of Christ, and secondly the Jewish and more particularly Palestinian features which abound in the synoptic gospels and make it impossible to regard them as the later creation of an almost entirely Hellenized church. It would be better if the present-day successors of

Couchoud and Alfaric were to stop going back to arguments as completely discredited as theirs. Even Soviet historians no longer really cling to them.

Unfortunately, Marc Stéphane,[32] Georges Ory[33] and some others continue to fly in the face of the evidence. They have recently received some support from England, where a scholar with some reputation in the field of the history of religion, John Allegro, has published a monumental book.[34] Its principal thesis is that Christianity is the resurgence of an ancient Mesopotamian cult based on the ecstasy produced by eating a sacred mushroom. The evidence for this theory, skilfully trimmed to suit the taste of the drug generation, is based on extravagant etymologies which are far from being convincing, though they would have to be overwhelmingly so to carry weight against much more probable constructions which pay attention to the content of the gospels and the earlier tradition.

It must be said, in face of the obstinate persistence of those who claim that Jesus is a myth, that the choice does not lie between the traditionalist biography of Jesus in its most conservative form and the mythological theories. The choice lies between the scholarly biography of the academic kind and an interpretation of the gospels as the vehicles of religious ideas, an interpretation which allows the personality of Jesus to drop into the background without burdening itself with a totally improbable theory. The traditionalist lives of Jesus and the works of those who deny his historical existence both lead to a dead end.

(b) The true heirs of D. F. Strauss are the theologians who reject all research into the biography of Jesus as doomed to failure and devoid of interest. The forceful manifesto published in 1892 by Martin Kähler entitled *Der sogenannte historische Jesus und der geschichtliche, biblische Christus*[35] was a sign that some theologians, much more conservative than Strauss, shared his view on this point. To his refusal to read the gospels as mere historical sources Kähler simply added an attachment to the person of Jesus Christ which was lacking in his predecessor.

This point of view remained an isolated one until it was taken up again by another group of inconoclasts, the advocates of dialectical theology, immediately after the First World War. Rudolf Bultmann became the most intransigent spokesman of the impossibility of writing any biography of Jesus and of reconstructing any more than the main outlines of his preaching. As a model of what was still possible, he published in 1926 his book *Jesus*,[36] which is more an interpretation of the message of its hero than an account of its content or a portrait of him. In the view of Bultmann and the other founders of the form-critical school, the gospels represent the writing down of an oral tradition which itself set out to interpret the person and message of Jesus for the purposes of preaching. Thus the student of New Testament theology can readily draw from these books information about the Christian *kerygma* in the last third of the first century, centred upon Christ and upon moral instruction. With somewhat more difficulty he can extract information about the faith of the Palestinian churches of the first generation which were the bearers of the synoptic tradition. Finally, he may attempt a somewhat hazardous reconstruction of the preaching of Jesus, based upon the few sayings amongst those attributed to him by the gospels which are probably authentic. If this outline is not to lack all interest, it must be intimately associated with an interpretation which is meaningful to modern man, an interpretation emphasizing the appeal to an existential decision.

Bultmann's *Jesus* remained an isolated phenomenon for about thirty years. After this demonstration, brilliant and yet disappointing, on the part of their leader, the colleagues and disciples of the great Marburg theologian turned their attention to other forms of research, and the flow of 'lives of Jesus' dried up almost entirely in German-speaking countries. The christology of the New Testament seemed entirely to have replaced the biography of Jesus, and those who thought it worth mentioning that the earthly existence of the Christ was of some importance for Christian faith gave the impression of being adherents of an old-fashioned liberal theology.

(c) However, in 1953 Ernst Käsemann, soon to be followed by numerous other disciples of Bultmann, raised the standard of revolt and dared to state that the knowledge of the historical Jesus was of interest for theology. This was the beginning of the movement which James M. Robinson in 1959 very aptly named *A New Quest of the Historical Jesus,* the title of his book published in that year.[37] There was an allusion here to the English title of Albert Schweitzer's great work, and Robinson's book was in fact aimed at showing the historical importance of the new school. Going much further than most of those who formed this movement, Robinson in effect claimed that the 'Life of Jesus' was at last emerging from the impasse into which Albert Schweitzer had led it.

He was not altogether wrong. No longer encumbered by its most ambitious objectives and its most irritating naïveties, but freed too from the inhibitions which had paralysed it for an entire generation, the study of the Jesus of history was able to return to life as a literary form. Thanks to the work of the form-critical school, it now possessed a much more precise tool for the analysis of the gospel texts than had been supplied by traditional literary criticism. At the same moment, the discoveries of Qumran and Nag Hammadi enlarged our knowledge of the surrounding environment in a promising way. The lively discussions that were taking place in Germany led one to hope that works of great value would result from them. Many articles in journals, as well as Robinson's work, seemed to promise this.

However, after almost twenty years of preparatory work, it must be admitted that the results are disappointing. Günther Bornkamm's *Jesus von Nazareth*[38] fills a gap, but it is not really a product of the new tendency, whatever its merits. A number of monographs on one aspect or another of the ministry of Jesus or of his message, and a number of brief introductions to the knowledge of his person, are no substitute for the scholarly and subtle works which the new school seemed to promise to German-speaking readers.

Although this school contains many scholars, it has produced only a single *Jesus,* that of Herbert Braun.[39] This is meant as a popular work, but the personality of its author, a left-wing disciple of Bultmann and an excellent writer, gives it a particular authority. In 160 small pages it presents the reader with an existentialist Jesus very similar to Bultmann's. Braun is rather less sceptical than his master with regard to the main outlines of the biography of Jesus, and rather more sceptical about the existence of God. This leads him to a good deal of fairly spectacular exegetical acrobatics. But there is one point on which Bultmann and Braun are in complete agreement: the incredible confidence with which they pronounce upon the authenticity of the sayings which the gospels place in the mouth of Jesus – after they have stated that in this field nothing is certain, but that enlightened specialists such as they must be trusted. In these circumstances, one is bound to admit that in German-speaking countries the 'new quest' has produced very disappointing results, even though the recent study by Jürgen Roloff, *Das Kerygma und der irdische Jesus*,[40] seems to represent a step forward.

It is perhaps in French-speaking countries that the 'new quest' has been most fruitful. First of all, one should mention the curious and attractive *Histoire de Jesus* by Arthur Nisin,[41] which is a brilliant attempt to draw all the consequences of the form-critical method for the knowledge of the person of the historical Jesus. More scholarly, more reasonable and better constructed, but also somewhat more 'heavy-footed', is the work by Xavier Léon-Dufour, *Les Evangiles et l'histoire de Jésus*.[42] His study of the gospels, then of the synoptic tradition, leads him to an interesting reconstruction of the life and message of Jesus which, while it makes considerable use of the results obtained in the preceding pages, unfortunately falls to some extent into a pattern borrowed from the most classical type of academic biography in respect of the chronological and topographical framework, and even of the main stages in the life of Jesus. One may also mention the recent short book by Michel Bouttier, *Du Christ de l'histoire au Jésus des Evangiles*,[43] which, though modest in appearance, shows very clearly where the problems of the life of Jesus lie in the post-Bultmann era.

It will be seen that none of this is very satisfying. It is surprising that the advocates of the 'new quest' have not achieved more convincing results and are marking time without any apparent reason. As this is due neither to a lack of knowledge nor to a lack of intelligence, one is led to wonder whether there is not some error of method. On reflection, there seem to be two. The first is that of not taking seriously historical works on the history of the redaction of the gospels, of which the first example was provided by Hans Conzelmann in 1954 with his *Die Mitte der Zeit*.[44] The second mistake consists in not taking any further the study of the oral tradition underlying the gospels, a study begun by the form-critical method, but rapidly broken off. It is clear that unless more attention is paid to the questions posed and the replies given by specialists in these two lines of research, no serious progress will be made in research into the life of Jesus, even by those who defend the most up-to-date types of this kind of literature.

2

The Gospels
and their Background

The interpretation given by the biographer of Jesus to the gospels necessarily has a decisive effect upon his work. The other documents which tell us about Jesus are no more than subsidiary sources, which have nothing essential to offer. It is therefore indispensable that there should be a link between the most up-to-date criticism of the gospels and studies of the person of Jesus himself. Among the gospels, Mark holds pride of place, since it is generally accepted as the first to have been written. The priority of Mark has been questioned in recent writings,[1] but the new arguments produced are not strong enough to challenge the accepted position.[2]

I

It is important, first, to note the large number of works bearing on the redaction of the synoptic gospels which have appeared since the publication of Conzelmann's pioneering book (see above, p. 12) in 1954. It is not necessary to give a complete list here. It is sufficient to mention, besides Conzelmann and Rigaux on Luke, Kilpatrick, Stendhal, Bornkamm, Trilling, Strecker and many others on Matthew, and Marxsen, Suhl, Tagawa and others on Mark.

There are numerous differences and even disagreements between these critics, with regard to both their results and their methods. But they are at one in their interest in the phenomenon of the redaction of a gospel and everything that accompanies it. They agree in considering that the way each evangelist chose the content of his work, ordered his material and handled the transitions between these passages reveals many features of his thought and characteristics of his background. The same is true, in the case of Matthew and Luke, of their way of correcting Mark. These critics almost all belong to the form-critical school, and consider that the various *pericopae* reached the evangelists in the form of isolated traditions or in small groups, and that the hand of the redactor is most clearly to be seen in the linking passages between them, and in their introductions and conclusions. Thus it is here above all that they look for the expression of the evangelist's own ideas.

In the eyes of these critics, the authors of the synoptic gospels are not great theologians. But because they belong to a church, and because their education is somewhat better than that of many of their fellow Christians, they are the spokesmen of their group, whose thought and religious outlook they reveal to us. Moreover, once their own thought has more or less been reconstructed, it is easier to discern the method by which they interpret the traditions and documents they use, and therefore to reconstruct the latter. This makes it possible to go further back, and with more accuracy, into the history of the synoptic tradition. In other words, a good 'redactional' study of the gospels ultimately brings us close to the historical Jesus, by making it easier for us to measure the stages through which we have to pass in working back from the gospel texts to Jesus himself.

In particular, such a study confirms the views of K. L. Schmidt on the subject of the chronological, topographical and even literary framework of the gospel. The late character of the whole framework linking together the *pericopae* is not merely the negative conclusion of a relentless historical criticism. It is also the positive result of a reconstruction of the thought and purpose of the writer. That is to say, by now it is an established fact, and any attempt to reconstruct the timetable and topographical sequence of the life of Jesus must avoid making a naïve use of what is suggested by the gospels. The sequences of events and place names that occur there were constructed, both in the tradition and in the canonical books, for practical or theological purposes. No biography of Jesus can any longer advance a chronological or topographical sequence based upon these texts. All that is possible is for a hypothetical

15

and provisional view to be put forward on the basis of the biographer's personal theory.

Some people may object that such a conclusion is not merely one of despair, but is an exaggeration, since the gospels contain precise topographical and chronological indications, in addition to those which are vague and can be interpreted as being given for symbolic or practical purposes. In fact there is no need to lapse into total scepticism. The use made of Galilee, Jerusalem, the 'Sea' of Tiberias, the desert and the 'desert places', etc., is normally symbolical; the chronological sequences are desperately vague ('In those days'; 'And then'; 'When Jesus had finished these sayings', etc.) or can sometimes be suspected of being symbolic in purpose because they are so surprisingly precise (the 'six days' of Mark 9.2, or the division of Mark 11–13 into days, for example). But there are also a good number of scattered statements that it would be wrong to suspect. They do not provide an itinerary of Jesus or a solution to the mystery of the duration of his public ministry. But they allow us to locate the latter in a more or less accurate way.

It was a wandering life, even though the stages in it did not follow each other as rapidly as the gospels suggest. We have no knowledge of its length, but it must certainly have been brief, even if the synoptic gospels do not succeed in convincing us that it lasted barely a single year. Certainly Jesus' activity in Galilee was considerable. We see him at Nazareth (Mark 6.1–6 par.; Luke 4.16–30), at Nain (Luke 7.11–17) and at Cana (John 2.1–11; 4.46–54), in the centre of Galilee and the tetrarchy of Philip, at Bethsaida (Matt. 11.12 par.; Mark 8.22; Luke 9.10), at Chorazin (Matt. 11.21 par.), at Dalmanutha (Mark 8.10), in the villages of the plain of Gennesaret (Mark 6.53ff. par.), in the country of the 'Gerasenes' (Mark 5.1 par.), at Magadan (Matt. 15.19). All these places are obscure or even impossible to identify, but the long list that one can make of them confirms what we already know from the numerous mentions of Capernaum, where Jesus seems to have had the use of a house, perhaps that of his disciple Simon Peter (Matt. 4.13; 8.5 par.; 11.23 par.; Mark 1.21 par.; 1.29 par.; 2.1; 3.20; 9.33; Luke 4.23; John 2.12; 6.17; 24, 59); at a certain time he even seems to have established his base there (Matt. 9.1). This tiny district, with its tropical micro-

climate, seems to have been a place which Jesus specially preferred, and we see him carrying out a varied and fruitful ministry there. Who can say why this man from the highlands, in
all probability coming from Nazareth (Matt. 2.23; 21.11;
Mark 1.9; Luke 2.39–51; John 1.45f.; Acts 10.38), chose this
particular region, where Jews and Gentiles lived side by side, as
the main location for his activity?

Elsewhere, we have few mentions of a journey through
Peraea (Mark 10.1 par.), but it is not impossible that Jesus
sometimes stayed in a place which the Fourth Gospel calls
Bethany (John 10.40; cf. John 11.7f.; 3.26; 1.28). His passage
through Samaria, mentioned by several texts (Luke 9.51–56;
17.11ff.), does not seem to have led to any lengthy stay. Jesus
travelled round and perhaps spent some time in a number
of regions bordering on Galilee in the north and the east of
this province (Mark 7.24, 31), but above all in the
'villages of Caesarea Philippi' below the foothills of Mount
Hermon (Mark 8.27 par.); all these regions had a Gentile
population and do not seem to have brought him any particular
success.

Finally, the topographical statements of the gospels, regard-
less of the symbolic elements which they contain, give evidence
of a certain activity of Jesus in Judaea. Jericho (Mark 10.46
par.; Luke 19.1), Ephraim on the edge of the desert (John
11.54), Bethphage (Mark 11.1 par.), Bethany (Mark 11.1 par.;
11.11f., par.; 14.3 par.; John 11.1,18; 12.1), and particularly
the latter, where Jesus had friends and returned several times,
were all visited by him. As for Jerusalem, for which the symbolic interpretation comes into play with particular intensity, it
is obvious that Jesus did not merely die there upon the cross, but
also came there two or three times as stated by the Fourth
Gospel (John 5.1; 7.14; 10.22). His activity there was certainly
quite intense; the synoptic gospels concentrate it into the days
preceding the Passion (Mark 11–13 par.) or locate it in other
places. We shall always remain ignorant of the length of these
stays and the intervals between them.

Studies of the redaction of the gospels leads to another problem, which most of the specialists who have discussed it have not
always understood quite correctly. However interesting the way
in which the evangelists went about the literary task they had

undertaken, it must not distract attention from the reason why they undertook it. The fact is that the churches of the first century and even those of the first half of the second century drew nourishment for their preaching from the great source of oral tradition, and in particular the synoptic tradition. H. Koester showed this clearly in 1957 in his book *Synoptische Überlieferung bei den apostolischen Vätern*,[3] and A. J. Bellinzoni confirmed it in 1967 in his study *The Sayings of Jesus in the Writings of Justin Martyr*.[4] Thus there was no obvious necessity for writing down gospels in order to gather together the content of this tradition. Why, then, did it take place?

As far as the gospels of Matthew and Luke are concerned, the question is less complex than in the case of the gospels of Mark and John. It is clear that the existence of the Gospel of Mark, which contained only part of the tradition known to the other two synoptic evangelists, was an encouragement to the latter to write in order to present readers with a more complete work, in which they would find the whole of the tradition. Of course, 'Matthew' and 'Luke' would have required other motivations as well. But their desire to integrate the whole content of the synoptic tradition into their work weighed heavily upon the plan of their books and upon the presentation which they made of the person and the work of Jesus: e.g. in the great discourses in Matthew which gather together everything about a particular subject, or the interminable narrative of the ascent to Jerusalem in Luke 9–18, etc.

The Gospel of John is too complex and too subtle a book to allow a brief explanation of the reason why it was written. It is frequently said that it is independent of the synoptic tradition and of the synoptic gospels. This thesis is, in our view, completely indefensible. The Fourth Gospel certainly made use of a very distinct tradition of its own, and in literary terms differs greatly from the synoptics. But would its choice of narratives and the style of its discourses have been the same without the deliberate intention of escaping from the mediocrity of the synoptic tradition? The miracle stories here are few in number, but always quite extraordinary, and are given a symbolic meaning which is always indicated or set out more or less at length. Are not these deliberately different from the many miraculous anecdotes, most of them fairly ordinary, which are piled up in Mark? The omnipotence of the Christ had to be demonstrated in a truly convincing fashion. As for the long and beautiful discourses spoken by Jesus in the Fourth Gospel, how can one suppose that they are not meant as an intentional contrast to the collections of mangled sayings, gathered into very artificial groups, which form the 'discourses' drawn from the tradition by the authors of the synoptic gospels (cf. Mark 9.33–50 par. or 13.1–37 par.)? In the opinion of 'John', Jesus spoke with majesty, and it was essential to let his readers feel this, instead of presenting them with strings of aphorisms with neither beginning nor end. Inspired by intentions of this kind, the author of the Fourth Gospel to some extent looked outside the synoptic tradition, which may have brought him several discoveries of interest for the biography of Jesus.[5] But it seems likely that he invented fairly freely the greater part of his work, or borrowed it from other religions. This is why one can rely on the Fourth Gospel only with the greatest care for documentation on the historical Jesus.

The delicate problem remains of the reason for the redaction of the Gospel of Mark, which has no known antecedent and which, because of its brevity and literary weaknesses, contains little within itself to show why it was written. For what reason, at a time when the only Christian writings were letters and perhaps a number of short handbooks gathering together the sayings of the Master on some subject or other of polemics or religious teaching, did a person choose to compose a semi-biographical narrative about Jesus – and not a work similar in nature to the *Rule* of Qumran, an apocalypse, a biblical commentary, or psalms? Why did such an original book use certain elements of the tradition which recorded sayings and acts of Jesus, while neglecting many more, including the most beautiful (the Beatitudes, the Lord's Prayer, numerous parables, etc.)? It is absurd to assume that Mark was ignorant of them, unless this explanation is limited to a few particular cases: all Christians prayed the Lord's Prayer, to take only one example. Furthermore, how did it come about that beside elements drawn from church tradition, the evangelist dared to place passages which, from their content, cannot be located within it, in particular several of the miracle stories (the possessed man at

Gerasa, the healings of the deaf and dumb man and the blind man at Bethsaida, etc.)?

We have discussed elsewhere the arguments on which a reply to these difficult questions can be based.[6] We shall do no more here than set out the solutions which seem to us to be the most probable. The Gospel of Mark is the work of a man who wished to reform the church of his time. He accuses it of neglecting its missionary duties and of complacently assuming a security guaranteed by the possession of the tradition which comes from Jesus. To this end, he appeals to history against tradition, and presents Christians with a portrait of Jesus where the whole emphasis is placed on the boldness, the mobility and the success of the missionary Master, whose vigour has not even been brought to an end by his Passion, since he has been raised from the dead, and his disciples continue his work. This portrait is never exclusively that of the historical Jesus. Like the tradition, it goes back to the historical Jesus, but it is valid for today, because the Christ is once again mysteriously present amongst his adherents. 'Mark' eliminates everything which, in the tradition, has no direct relevance to his aim. He preserves all that can be integrated into his argument, but sometimes boldly corrects it, so obliging the other evangelists to restore the primitive form in a number of cases. In order the better to shake the false self-confidence of the official guardians of church tradition, he went outside it for narratives concerning Jesus, and found them above all in the very region of Jesus' activity, in the villages round Lake Tiberias, where the famous healer of the past was still spoken of. In short, he took bold initiatives which make his book a precious source for the biography of Jesus, but one which is far from being the naïve description, without any very clear theological tendency, which it has sometimes been called. This at least is the conclusion of studies of the redaction of Mark.

The biographer of Jesus can therefore use all four gospels, but principally the synoptics. Amongst these, he will give priority to Mark, but will sometimes prefer one of the others, when Mark has ignored or modified important facts.

II

The other interesting innovation in the criticism of the gospels during the last fifteen years has been a return to the discussion of the oral tradition preceding the gospels. The form-critical school never took the trouble to define very precisely the concept of tradition which was implicit in its early publications. For almost all the representatives of this school, it is a somewhat vague notion of a general sociological nature. The Christian community, it was thought, had stored up a certain number of short narratives and brief collections of sayings to satisfy the needs of its collective existence. Dibelius considered that the primary motive had been the needs of missionary preaching, followed by that of a taste for good stories which was displayed by the second generation, and is nothing unusual in so popular a setting. But his classification is unsatisfactory. Bultmann related the numerous categories of words of Jesus which he had identified to various activities of the primitive church: teaching, preaching, controversy and confessions of faith. But this link was regarded by him principally as an explanation of the *creation* of each unit of tradition. The community, he considered, played a very active role in this respect, even with regard to units containing an authentic kernel. What is lacking in this theory is a study of conditions of *transmission*, as well as an effort to state clearly the problem of the starting point of the tradition concerning Jesus. As in the case of Dibelius, the community is thought of as endowed with great creative powers, and the essential law governing the transmission of the tradition seems to be that of rapid change.

Many voices were raised between 1920 and 1940 criticizing the inadequacies of the thesis, so convincing in other respects, that the synoptic gospels were constructed by placing end to end small units derived from the oral tradition which was used by the churches for practical purposes. However, the form-critical school found its methods increasingly adopted without having to take account of these objections. A few isolated scholars, the most interesting of them being Marcel Jousse, tried to interest New Testament specialists in the technical problem of the transmission of traditions.[7] Yet in spite of the interest that Alfred Loisy took in this work, and the high regard in which Maurice Goguel held it, the theses of Jousse did not achieve the success which, in spite of some of their extreme features, they deserved. This is to be regretted, because he gave a vigorous demonstration that the striking rhythm of many of the sayings attributed to Jesus by the gospels was due to the systematic use in oral tradition, from the Aramaic stage on, of mnemonic devices such as repetition, antithesis and balance. Drawing on numerous parallels, Jousse also showed the extraordinary stability of an oral tradition memorized in a systematic fashion amongst people for whom books are still luxury objects. Thus the form-critical thesis of the extreme flexibility of the synoptic tradition was seriously shaken.

However, it was not until 1957 that the ideas of the form-critical school about the tradition were once again radically criticized, and a genuine discussion took place. A lecture given that year in Oxford by Harald Riesenfeld formed the manifesto of the new movement.[8] Riesenfeld maintained that the only possible origin of the synoptic tradition was the teaching given by Jesus to his disciples and memorized by them on his orders in the same way as was done in the rabbinic schools of the time. Thanks to the use of mnemonic devices and the powers of the human memory, the words of Jesus, and those of his acts which he intended to be handed down to the generations to come in the form of an official narrative, are known to us, Riesenfeld claimed, with great accuracy, in spite of a few distortions due to translation into Greek and the redaction of the gospels. One could not wish for anything more positive and provocative.

The debate which Riesenfeld wished for was soon under way. There were numerous contributors to it, amongst whom the following may be mentioned: T. Boman, G. Delling, B. Gerhardsson, H. Schürmann, G. Vermès, G. Widengren. Most of these critics dissociated themselves from the most radical theses of Riesenfeld and his disciple Gerhardsson. But the attack on the improbability of the form-critical conception of the gospel tradition had hit the mark, and various attempts have been made to put forward a more satisfying theory. Three examples are worth mentioning here.

The first of these is no more than an article published in Berlin in 1960 in a large symposium on Jesus.[9] It was written by a German Catholic scholar, H. Schürmann, who set out to consider 'The Pre-paschal Origins of the Tradition of the *Logia*', with the sub-title: 'An Essay in a Form-Critical Approach to the Life of Jesus'.[10] These closely-packed pages are extremely important. Schürmann emphasizes that, while the *Sitz im Leben* of the tradition of the words of Jesus is difficult to locate in the primitive church, there is an obvious place for it in the life of the group of disciples gathered round their Master. This group shared a certain community life and took part in missionary preaching. The *logia* of Jesus can easily be divided into rules concerning community life and sayings intended to organize and nourish missionary preaching.

We shall return to this very suggestive study. Let us for the moment say only that Schürmann has a tendency to apply his argument to texts to which it is not quite as appropriate as to the sayings and exhortations, such as the parables and many of the conflict narratives. But he is certainly right in regard to the rest, which, in spite of later distortions, give some hope to the biographer of Jesus of being able to reconstruct at least the relationship between Jesus and his disciples.

Another attempt is that of Lucien Cerfaux, who, after numerous preliminary studies, published in 1968 a book entitled *Jésus aux origines de la tradition, matériaux pour l'histoire évangélique*.[11] This is of real interest, even if one might hesitate to follow most of his arguments to their conclusion. Cerfaux recognizes that it is not satisfactory to talk of a single synoptic tradition, since there are so many differences between the various elements which form it. He identifies four traditions, the two principal ones being the Galilean and the Jerusalem traditions, while the two others are the tradition of the 'disciples' and that of the '*logia* of the Lord'. He regards the Galilean tradition as having been principally the vehicle of the message of the kingdom of God (especially the discourses of Jesus and the parables of the kingdom) and the miracle and conflict stories. That of Jerusalem consisted of all the preludes to the passion, and the passion narrative itself. The tradition 'of the disciples' consists essentially of the content of the 'great interpolation' of Luke 9–18. Finally, the tradition of the *logia* contained all the isolated statements, those which formed the point of a condensed narrative (the paradigms of Dibelius) and those which the tradition was beginning to gather into collections, even though they did not form a true discourse. The main weakness of this sub-division is that according to Cerfaux it does not correspond to different settings for the transmission of each distinct tradition. However, there are exceptions to this rule (cf. the statements on p. 142 about the transmission of the conflict narratives).

Thus one can at least accept from Cerfaux's imperfect essay his conclusion that the synoptic tradition is unquestionably less monolithic than has sometimes been supposed, both by form-critics and by their opponents, as for example by Riesenfeld. Certain of its elements may well have been handed down in different settings.

Finally, one must mention the important studies of Joachim Jeremias, who, like Cerfaux, has for a long time been carrying out a very personal inquiry into the transmission of the words of Jesus. He refuses to acknowledge the creative force of oral tradition, even though he agrees with most of the other theses of the form-critical school. We shall return later to some of his works. The most authoritative of these is his *New Testament Theology*,[12] which, after a profound critical analysis of all the documentary evidence, and after taking into account the distortions which have affected the sayings of Jesus in the course of transmission, proposes a very interesting reconstruction of Jesus' preaching. In our view the criteria of authenticity with which Jeremias works are more fragile than he maintains, and the interpretation which he gives of the message of Jesus is too systematic to be convincing. But one can agree with him that oral tradition is much more faithful than it is sometimes said to be; that there is no question that its source is Jesus himself; and that it is possible with the aid of this tradition to go back to Jesus behind the primitive church.

There is no sign that reflection on the synoptic tradition has yet come to an end. Let us, however, outline a few provisional conclusions, which will be of value to us in our quest of the historical Jesus.

First of all, since the redactional activity of the gospel writers was greater than used to be supposed, and the stability of the tradition was greater than the form-critical school claimed, many of the changes within the tradition must be located at the stage when it was committed to writing. The passage from Aramaic to Greek often caused earlier modifications, but whenever the oral tradition was organized it did not allow very considerable changes, even in the course of translation.

Secondly, the activity of the evangelists in collecting material seems to have been more considerable than used to be maintained. In other words, each of them gathered documents from various sources, certain of which may not perhaps have had any connection with the church traditions which supplied the bulk of their material. These documents were virtually all oral and were handed down according to the rules of popular memorized tradition, in a variety of ways.

The origin of those of the traditions which seem to have been handed down in an organized and systematic way (isolated sayings and the kernels of discourses) can be sought in the initiative of the historical Jesus, who imposed on his disciples the memorizing of these traditions to train them in community life and missionary preaching. Thus generally these texts are excellent sources for the knowledge of Jesus.

In the case of the more flexible traditions, the first initiative was taken by various people or groups whose preoccupations, culture and intentions have left their mark on the texts. These groups were occasionally capable of creating anecdotes or sayings of the Lord for their own needs. As a general rule, they took as their starting point authentic memories of the activity of Jesus, which they transformed to a greater or lesser degree. Consequently, these texts give us the impression such persons or groups had of the Master, rather than reliable information about his person.

Thus we must make an inventory of the 'portraits' of Jesus with which we are provided by the tradition underlying the gospels. This inventory must begin with the portrait of the Master which the disciples handed down in the form of a rigorously memorized tradition. But although this is unquestionably more faithful than the others, we shall see that it is very far from being all the truth about him.

Then we shall have to ask whether the gospels tell us anything about yet other portraits of Jesus: those of the groups who had dealings with him when he was alive, but did not create any tradition concerning him. Finally, we must attempt a partial synthesis of these various portraits in order to present a coherent picture of Jesus. This operation is extremely risky, and to a considerable extent is arbitrary. But it may help us in the end to make Jesus comprehensible to modern minds, which in our view justifies the risks.

Before beginning this inventory of portraits of Jesus, let us say which gospel texts will not be considered in our study because they teach us nothing, or almost nothing, about the historical Jesus. The first of these are the infancy narratives in the gospels of Matthew and Luke, which may contain some indications about the origins of Jesus, but are not a tradition of the family into which he was born, contrary to what Cardinal Daniélou has recently stated (cf. above p. 5). These narratives are legends dating from almost half a century after the death of Jesus, and tell us about the christology of the years AD 80–90. Secondly, we shall set aside all the narratives of appearances of the risen Christ contained in the gospels of Matthew, Luke and John. These are later anecdotes, the starting point of which was the list of appearances given by Paul in I Cor. 15.5ff. It seems that at first there was a refusal to describe these christophanies publicly, and that half a century later the necessary steps were taken to fill what was by then regarded as a gap. Finally, we shall not consider the discourses in the Fourth Gospel, which of course may contain some echoes of the words of the historical Jesus, but which the Johannine milieu and the evangelist himself constructed on the basis of their meditations. They bring us a christology of incalculable richness, as does the prologue. But they hardly bring us any closer to Jesus of Nazareth. On the other hand, the narratives in the Fourth Gospel give us some details of the impression Jesus made upon certain groups, and we shall therefore take them into account.

26

3

The Jesus of the
'Dominical Sayings'

The Greek term *logia* is often used to refer to the sayings of
Jesus, since it was applied by Papias of Hierapolis in the second
century to the content of the collection which he attributed to
Matthew. But it has been used by scholars with such varying
meanings that it is better to substitute for it an expression like
'dominical sayings' to describe the elements of the tradition
which we are now going to examine. These are isolated sayings,
and groups of sayings of Jesus, which neither include nor ac-
company a narrative.

These statements by Jesus are simply introduced in the synoptic gospel by brief formulae such as 'And he said to
them', sometimes extended by one or two brief sentences specify-
ing the date, the place and those addressed (e.g. Matt. 5.1f.).
They are sometimes followed by one or two sentences which
note the effect produced or the repetition of the teaching
in question: e.g. Mark 4.33f. and the conclusions of the
discourses in the Gospel of Matthew. These introductions
and conclusions are very largely the work of the evangelists,
although very simple introductions like 'Jesus said' must
certainly have accompanied some of the sayings in the
tradition.

In his *The History of the Synoptic Tradition*,[1] Rudolf
Bultmann subdivided the dominical sayings into five categories:
the *logia* in the narrower sense, wisdom-sayings; prophetic and
apocalyptic sayings; legal sayings and community regulations;
'I-sayings'; parables and related material. We shall not discuss
here the last category, which we shall study later, for the simple
reason that its form is very different and does not include the

rhythm which is so striking a characteristic of the other sayings of the Lord.

This is not the place to go over the whole excellent inventory which Bultmann has made of this group of traditions. We must, however, give a few characteristic examples of the sayings in each of the four categories mentioned above, before going on to the question of what they teach us of the Jesus of history.

Like the *māshāl* in Hebrew literature, the *logion* may vary greatly in form. It may state a principle, like a proverb. When it does, the subject of the action may be a thing, as in Mark 4.22 par.:

> For there is nothing hid,
> except to be made manifest;
> nor is anything secret,
> except to come to light.

Or it may give this role to a person, as in Matt. 12.30 par.:

> He who is not with me
> is against me,
> and he who does not gather with me,
> scatters.

The same is found again in Matt. 8.20 par.:

> Foxes have holes,
> and the birds of the air have nests;
> but the Son of man has nowhere
> to lay his head.

Other *logia* are exhortations in the imperative, as in Matt. 8.22 par.:

> Leave the dead to bury their own dead.

Or in Mark 9.43–47 par.:

> If your hand causes you to sin, cut it off;
> it is better for you to enter life maimed
> than with two hands to go to hell,
> to the unquenchable fire.
> And if your foot causes you to sin, cut it off;
> it is better for you to enter life lame
> than with two feet to be thrown into hell.

And if your eye causes you to sin, pluck it out;
it is better for you to enter the kingdom of God with one
eye
than with two eyes to be thrown into hell.

The *logion* may also be formulated as a question, as in
Matt. 6.27 par.:

Which of you by being anxious can add one cubit to his
stature?

Finally, we find collections of *logia* consisting of sayings in
two or more of the forms mentioned above, as in Matt. 7.7–11
par.:

Ask, and it will be given you;
seek and you will find;
knock, and it will be opened to you.
For everyone who asks receives,
and he who seeks finds,
and to him who knocks it will be opened.
Or what man of you, if his son asks him for bread,
will give him a stone?
Or if he asks for a fish,
will give him a serpent?
If you, then, who are evil, know how to give good gifts to
your children,
How much more will your Father who is in heaven give good
things to those who ask him?

Such collections go back to the origins of the tradition, while
others are more recent. The proof is found in the perfect paral-
lelism between the gospels with regard to the oldest collections.

The *prophetic and apocalyptic sayings* which – curiously
enough – contain virtually no mention of visions which Jesus
may have had (though cf. Luke 10.18) can be divided into four
categories. There are first of all the promises of salvation, the
best example of which is the collection of the Beatitudes (Matt.
5.3–12 and Luke 6.20–23). One may also mention Mark 8.35
par.:

Whoever would save his life will lose it;

29

and whoever loses his life for my sake and the gospel's
will save it.

Then there are the prophetic threats, of which the woes on
the rich, Luke 6.25f., are a particularly striking case. One may
also mention Matt. 7.22f. par.:

On that day many will say to me, 'Lord, Lord, did we not
prophesy in your name, and cast out demons in your
name, and do many mighty works in your name?' And then
will I declare to them, 'I never knew you; depart from me,
you evildoers.'

The prophetic admonitions form another rather different
category. Let us quote, in addition to a certain number of
parables which we will study below, the summary of the
preaching of Jesus found in Mark 1.15 (and Matt. 4.17, in an
abbreviated form):

The time is fulfilled, and the kingdom of God is at hand;
Repent, and believe in the gospel.

Finally, there are the apocalytic predictions, amongst which
can be included for example virtually the whole of Mark 13
and its parallels, or the portrayal of the last judgment in Matt.
25.31–46.

Amongst the *legal sayings and community regulations*, it is
more difficult to pick out clear categories, although there is a
great variety. Let us simply quote some characteristic
examples:

Mark 10.11–12: Whoever divorces his wife and marries
another, commits adultery against her; and if she divorces
her husband and marries another, she commits adultery.

Matt. 5. 21f.: You have heard that it was said to the men of
old, 'You shall not kill; and whoever kills shall be liable to
judgment'. But I say to you that everyone who is angry with
his brother shall be liable to judgment; whoever insults his
brother shall be liable to the council, and whoever says, 'You
fool!', shall be liable to the hell of fire.

Matt. 16.18f.: You are Peter, and on this rock I will build my church, and the powers of death shall not prevail against it. I will give you the keys of the kingdom of heaven, and whatever you bind on earth shall be bound in heaven, and whatever you loose on earth shall be loosed in heaven.

Mark 6.8–11. par.: He charged them to take nothing for their journey except a staff; no bread, no bag, no money in their belts; but to wear sandals and 'Do not put on two tunics'. And he said to them, 'Where you enter a house, stay there until you leave the place. And if any place will not receive you and they refuse to hear you, when you leave, shake off the dust that is on your feet for a testimony against them.'

Finally, there are the 'I-sayings', sayings in the first person singular, a certain number of which are to be found in the preceding groups. One may naturally associate with them certain of the sayings concerning the Son of man peculiar to Matthew, since in the eyes of that evangelist the identity between Jesus and the Son of man was total. The first group is formed by the passages in which Jesus speaks of his coming, as in Mark 2.17:

I came not to call the righteous, but sinners.

Or there is Luke 12.49f.:

I came to cast fire upon the earth;
and would that it were already kindled!
I have a baptism to be baptized with;
and how I am constrained until it is accomplished!

Finally, there is Matt. 10.40:

He who receives you receives me,
and he who receives me receives him who sent me.

Another group, the boundaries of which are admittedly rather vague, is comprised of sayings in which Jesus speaks in the first person singular without referring to his coming. The celebrated declaration in Matt. 11.25–30, with its partial parallel in Luke 10.21f., is the most striking example of this type of dominical saying:

I thank thee, Father, Lord of heaven and earth, that thou

31

hast hidden these things from the wise and understanding and revealed them to babes; yea, Father, for such was thy gracious will. All things have been delivered to me by my Father; and no one knows the Son except the Father, and no one knows the Father except the Son and any one to whom the Son chooses to reveal him. Come to me, all who labour and are heavy laden, and I will give you rest. Take my yoke upon you, and learn from me; for I am gentle and lowly in heart, and you will find rest for your souls. For my yoke is easy, and my burden is light.

There are less astounding sayings which belong to the same group, such as Luke 11.20 par.:

But if it is by the finger of God that I cast out demons,
then the kingdom of God has come upon you.

Again, there is Luke 14.27 par.:

Whoever does not bear his own cross and come after me, cannot be my disciple.

We will not follow Bultmann in his attempt to identify a particular evolution of the tradition for each of the classes of saying as defined above. We believe that this undertaking is bound to fail, even if it is regarded as useful. In fact these categories differ from each other more by their subject than by their form, and there are in addition appreciable differences within each category, in respect of both form and content. Our information on the primitive church does not allow us to distinguish the different tendencies which may have influenced groups of sayings which are too few in number. We must restrict ourselves to observations on numerous and relatively extensive texts, that is, in the circumstances, on the total category of dominical sayings.

The simplest solution would apparently be to accept the authenticity of the whole of the dominical sayings and to use these sayings to reconstruct the message of the historical Jesus. But the difficulties appear at once, even if one has a favourable prejudice towards a tradition so evidently intended to be memorized.

There are, to begin with, serious divergencies between the three synoptic gospels in respect of many of these sayings. When

32

Mark carries a saying which Matthew or Luke, or one of them, present in a different form, there are cases where he seems to give the oldest form. But there are quite a few others where one has the impression that he has improved on the tradition, while Matthew and Luke, or one of them, have returned to it; for they knew it as well as Mark (Mark 8.35 par.; 10.12 par.; etc.). If a saying is found only in Matthew and Luke, with a different form in each, which is the oldest text (cf. Matt. 12. 28 and Luke 11.9; the Beatitudes in Matt. 5 and Luke 6, etc.)? Finally, when a saying is found in only one of the gospels, can we be sure that it was not the work of that gospel writer at the moment of the redaction of his book (cf. Mark 2.27; Matt. 7.15; 16.17–19; Luke 12.47f.; etc)? It is obvious that a choice often has to be made, and the profound difference between critics on these questions show that there is no satisfactory criterion for making these choices.

It is not just a question of going back to the tradition behind the redaction. It seems likely that certain sayings were introduced into the tradition even before the gospels were written down. There is every likelihood that the words of the risen Christ quoted by the gospels are neither inventions of the evangelists nor sayings of the historical Jesus transferred to this context. Sayings such as Matt. 28.18–20 or Luke 24.49 were no doubt heard in the course of christophanies or ecstatic phenomena. But if this is so, what of a certain number of very similar sayings which Jesus is presented as uttering before his crucifixion (Matt. 18.20, for example)? What is the boundary between such cases and those where the speaker was the historical Jesus, with an authority which is certainly astonishing, but which there is no proof that he did not claim? Here again, the criteria are difficult to establish, to judge by the disagreements between scholars.

Sayings in the first person singular may have multiplied in the post-paschal tradition, because this is a form particularly suited to the inspired declarations of prophets seized by the Spirit and speaking in the name of the Lord. But Christians had been warned to mistrust declarations of this kind (Mark 13.6 par.), and it would be a bold claim that the historical Jesus never employed this style in his instructions to his disciples. Thus it must be allowed that the same is true of his sayings in

33

the first person singular as of the other sayings of the Lord, that what goes back to the historical Jesus and what does not derive from him are so closely entangled that it is impossible for us to separate them.

The same is true of all the sayings in which Jesus uses the expression 'Son of man'. The authenticity of all these statements has sometimes been disputed, on the strength of the argument that the idea of the Son of man is incompatible with that of the kingdom of God.[2] We are so uncertain of the meaning of these two expressions at various stages in the oral tradition and the redaction of the gospels that this thesis is almost ludicrous. But it is quite evident that either a late stage of the tradition or the evangelists Matthew and Luke had a tendency to introduce the title Son of man into numerous dominical sayings to replace the first person singular – and the reverse also took place (cf. Matt. 10.32 and Luke 12.8; Matt 16.21 par.; Matt. 19.28 and Luke 22.28; Matt. 20.28 par.; etc.). This is evidence of a certain amount of confusion in the documents which make the tradition known to us. This confusion is explicable in view of the mysterious nature of the title in question, which is connected with more or less esoteric speculations (cf. Dan. 7 and I Enoch) which were clearly no longer known to the second Christian generation. But again, where are the boundaries between authentic sayings mentioning the Son of man, sayings coloured by the Passion and the Resurrection, sayings created by the primitive church and later passages where the phrase is no longer anything but a way in which Jesus says 'I'? Scholars dispute about this, often heatedly, and a great variety of systems has been put forward. But it is clear that the intermingling is too great for it to be possible to separate these different strata completely. They are all found within each of the three groups of dominical sayings which mention the Son of man: those which concern his earthly life (e.g. Mark 2.10 par.); those mentioning his suffering (e.g. Mark 8.31 par.); and those which mention his role as the eschatological judge (e.g. Mark 8.38 par.). In face of this situation, the impossibility of making reliable decisions about the problems of authenticity is best recognized, and another way sought.

The same difficulty is found with the dominical sayings which are calls to missionary preaching and regulations for community life. It is obvious that Matthew 10 and 18 are compilations of elements which had been only partially gathered together by the tradition, to judge by the parallel passages in Luke. Matthew certainly varied some of these sayings during the redaction of these two chapters, in order to take account of the situation of the church of his time. But the earlier oral tradition no doubt already reflected a first attempt to systematize them and adapt them to the realities of the church at that time. Apart from this, the tradition which was the vehicle of most of these sayings goes back to a large degree to the instructions given by Jesus to his disciples, because situations of this kind had existed amongst them from the period when their Master gathered them together and sent them out into the field to preach and heal the sick. How can one distinguish between what comes from each of these three sources, when we know little or nothing about the characteristics of the life of the group at each of these three stages, and when we have to admit in any case that the tradition was relatively fixed? We are afraid that many of the judgments made by critics on this issue are totally arbitrary, and collapse as soon as the idea of the community creating the tradition is called into question.

Thus we face a dilemma. It is impossible to reconstruct the teaching of Jesus by using all the dominical sayings. But it is impossible to disentangle them in such a way as to provide a sounder basis. Some critics, of course, believe it possible, using formal characteristics alone, to distinguish certain sayings of indisputable authenticity, on the basis of which all the others can be judged. But even the characteristics of the *ipsissima verba Jesu*, as Joachim Jeremias defined them in 1953, as in the expression 'Amen, I say to you . . .', are understood by others[3] as indicating that these sayings are revelations derived from the risen Christ and transmitted by Christian prophets. Thus it would be imprudent to make such isolated sayings the basis for the whole reconstruction of the teaching of Jesus.

We may add that because of their paradoxical nature, the brevity of many of them, and the frequent translation errors which can be observed or suspected in them, the dominical sayings are often obscure and sometimes totally incomprehensible (Mark 9.49; Matt. 11.12 par.; Luke 17.20f., for example). Separated from the context in which they were

35

uttered and from that in which they were memorized, they are scattered pearls which no longer allow the reconstruction of a coherent whole. In short, these sayings give us no more than distant and limited hints about the teaching of the historical Jesus.

Must we, then, abandon our search? We do not think so. We have to look for the narrow and tortuous way which leads out of the impasse.

This route can be followed by way of a study of the totality of the dominical sayings, and leads us not to an exact account of the teaching of Jesus, which is virtually impossible to reconstruct with the least degree of certainty, but to the *total impression made by the Master on his disciples*, who were the privileged hearers of these sayings, which were meant to be memorized. Of course a study of this kind does not allow a clear distinction between the portrait of Jesus which his disciples had of him when he was alive and that which those who carried on the tradition had in the course of the two next generations. But we shall see that there is, corresponding to the generally fixed and stable form of this type of memorized tradition, a real stability in the portrait of Jesus of which it is the vehicle, even though this portrait has undergone modifications in matters of detail.

The historical Jesus was surrounded by a group of men who shared his life at least during part of his public ministry. Objections can be raised against the historicity of a certain number of stories concerning the disciples in the gospels, whether these are narratives of their call (Mark 1.16–20 par.; Luke 5.1–11; Mark 2.14 par.); passages listing the Twelve, beginning with the narrative of their calling (Mark 3.13–19 par.); the mentions of the title 'apostle' (e.g. Luke 6.13); or the particular promises made to Peter (Matt 16.18f.). Even supposing that all these objections are well founded, which is far from being obvious, they would not cast doubt on the historical existence of the group of companions of Jesus. The texts are too numerous, too various, and too probable – in short, too compelling.

Some critics argue from the fact that the companions of Jesus are constantly described in the gospels as 'disciples', and liken them to the pupils which the rabbis of the period taught at home, trained at length and burdened with all sorts of humble tasks (so Riesenfeld, Gerhardsson, etc.). Their thesis is reinforced by the existence behind the gospels of a carefully memorized oral tradition, comparable in many points to that of the rabbinic schools. Nevertheless, Jesus was not a rabbi in the precise sense of the term, if only on account of his wanderings and his total independence of earlier masters, which was inconceivable for anyone with a rabbinic cast of mind. As for his disciples, they differed profoundly from the pupils of the rabbis by the much less scholarly nature of their behaviour and their greater activity, if we are to believe the total impression given by the gospels.

Nor can the group of companions of Jesus be likened to a religious community like that of Qumran or the other Essenizing or baptizing brotherhoods which seem to have been fairly numerous in the Palestine of that period. It is likely that they were influenced from this direction, but the small group that surrounded Jesus did not have the rigid discipline, the long admission procedures, the exclusiveness and the clericalism of the Essenes. Even though there must have been aspects of their common existence about which we know nothing, there was certainly not sufficient time before the crucifixion of Jesus for them to organize it, and they developed neither stability in one place nor an ascetic sense (cf. for example Mark 2.18ff. par.; Matt. 11.16–19 par.).

Nor does a comparison with the group of disciples of John the Baptist supply us with the key to the constitution of the band of companions of Jesus. This is so first of all because we know very little about the Baptist's disciples; but also because the asceticism of the baptizers was in strong contrast to the very liberal attitude of Jesus and his disciples (cf. the two texts just quoted). And yet there are features common to both groups: their itinerant life, their general appeal to repentance motivated by imminent eschatological beliefs, the practice of a single baptism, and perhaps also the handing down of a tradition, since there certainly existed a Baptist tradition of which traces are preserved in the early chapters of the Fourth Gospel, as in the passages of the synoptic gospels which record the preaching of John the Baptist (Luke 3.7–18 par.).

To sum up, the group of disciples of Jesus seems to have been a distinct and unique entity, a kind of brotherhood of healing preachers who divided their time between training by their founder and activity in the field (Mark 3.14f.; 6.7–13). The tradition of the dominical sayings must be placed in this setting, as has been clearly shown by H. Schürmann in the article quoted above pp. 22f.).

Many of these sayings have a direct relationship with the preaching activity of Jesus' companions. Their rhythmic and symmetrical form, intended to make them easier to memorize, no doubt has another aim beside that. It is also meant to make preaching and teaching easier for those who went on tour. Since the preaching dealt in particular with the imminence of the end and the coming of the kingdom of God, the sayings concerning these subjects find their places here: Luke 6.20f. (Beatitudes); 10.23f.; 12.54f.; Mark 13.28f. (signs of the times); Luke 17.34f. (the suddenness of the end); Luke 11.20 and Mark 3.27 (miracles as signs of the kingdom); Matt. 11.2–6 and Luke 7.18–23 (the sending of the disciples); etc.

The sayings which are above all appeals for conversion are also amongst those which the disciples received from Jesus as material for their own preaching; calls for understanding and decision (Matt. 7.19; Mark 9.43 par.; Matt. 24.37–39); calls for vigilance (Luke 12.39f.; Mark 13.35f.); warnings to Israel (Luke 13.1–5; 4.25–27); etc.

The sayings concerning the law of Moses and the tradition of the Pharisees would also have been very useful for preachers whose hearers were almost exclusively Jews (Matt. 10.5f.): for example, the greater part of Matthew 5 and 6. The moral teaching which Jesus gave in certain of these sayings was also wholly suitable for the disciples' preaching: on poverty (Matt. 6.19f., 24); on forgiveness (Matt. 5.23f.; Luke 17.3f.); and on loving one's enemies (Matt 5.38–48, in part at least). There are many other examples of dominical sayings intended to guide, illustrate and impress upon the minds of the hearers the preaching of Jesus' companions. Their use only in Jesus' own preaching would not have ensured their preservation, and in fact this was made possible only because they were memorized by the disciples for the purposes of their preaching ministry.

The purpose of other dominical sayings is the development of concord and community life amongst the disciples, although they never take on the appearance of a rule comparable to that of Qumran. In this way Jesus emphasizes what it means to be a disciple; the prohibition of any relaxation of zeal (Luke 14.26; 9.60–62); an arduous and simple life (Mark 8.34f. and 10.29f. par.); particular promises made to the disciples (Mark 10.28f.; Luke 22.28–30; etc.). The material difficulties of the disciples are often mentioned in terms which the later situation would no longer have justified to the same extent: the renunciation of all material security based on earnings (Matt. 6.34; Luke 12.22–31) or on possessions (Luke 12.33 and Mark 10.21); rules concerning the itinerant life (Luke 10.4–7; Mark 9.41); etc. There are also sayings which serve as rules for community life: for example, the obligation to be the servant of all (Mark 9.35; 10.42–45 par.).

The authenticity of the sayings we have quoted in the previous paragraph is accepted by most critics, and we have quoted only such sayings in order to make it clear that the original *Sitz im Leben* of the dominical sayings is the calling together and sending out of the disciples, and not the catechesis of the later church. But, as we have emphasized above, the boundary between what is 'authentic' and what is 'unauthentic' is so fluid that this conclusion must be applied to the *whole body* of all the dominical sayings. On the other hand, it must be accepted that in this group of traditions we can look only for the general impression which Jesus made upon his disciples.

It has frequently been stated that Jesus was regarded by his companions as a rabbi, even though he did not make them his pupils in the usual manner of that period. What we have said above makes it unnecessary for us to enlarge on the reasons that make this hypothesis improbable. Of course Jesus is sometimes called *rabbi* (Mark 9.5; 14.45 par.; John 1.38–49; 3.2; etc.) or *rabbouni* (Mark 10.51; John 20.16). But in the first century AD these terms do not yet have the precise meaning of a master whose task is to teach the law and the oral tradition which they came to have later. They were at that time, in the gospels as in the Judaism of the period, no more than extremely respectful titles, which the Greek readily translates as *kyrie* (Matt. 10.33; 17.4; Luke 8.41) or *epistata* (Luke 9.33), even though the translation *didaskale*, 'teacher', found favour with others (John 1.38; 20.16).

The comparative frequency of this last word, which is particularly striking in the Gospel of Mark, does, however, suggest that Jesus was understood and presented by his disciples as a 'teacher', a person of whom teaching was the main characteristic. But this Master, who 'teaches' in so many passages, is not, like the rabbis, a member of a corporate body in which the essential value is continuity. He is much more like the 'Teacher of Righteousness' in Qumran, chosen by God at the end of time to teach Israel the 'last commandments' and to reveal to Israel the mysteries of the divine activity and the eschatological judgment. Like the Teacher of Righteousness, he teaches what he receives directly from God with a personal authority which found no parallel amongst the 'scribes' (cf. Mark 2.21f.).

The dominical sayings handed down by the tradition give very impressive examples of the authority which Jesus displayed. The antitheses of the Sermon on the Mount (Matt. 5.21–48), the sayings concerning what is clean and unclean (Mark 7.14f. par.), many of the statements denouncing the errors of the 'scribes and Pharisees, hypocrites' (Matt. 23 par.), show that he adopted an attitude of radical freedom towards the oral tradition of the Pharisees, and that this boldness sometimes extended to the very letter of the law (Mark 7.15). He showed an authoritative readiness to give a completely personal interpretation of the law. The disciples who were attracted to this Master certainly did not have the same impression of him as the pupils of the 'teachers of the law', with their boundless respect for the letter and their unconditional devotion to the oral tradition, which they regarded as going back to the revelation of Sinai. Matthew 11.28–30 is an impressive confirmation of this.

There is no question that the unique authority which Jesus enjoyed with his disciples was due in part to his personal 'wisdom'. This is admirably illustrated by many of the *logia*, which display a remarkable gift of expression which make Jesus the equal of the most brilliant wisdom writers. The companions of Jesus seem to have been simple, though neither stupid or uncultivated, and by all appearances they seem to have been impressed by this talent for finding the right phrase. Is there any better proof of this than the astounding result that the tradition attributes to the saying: 'I will make you fishers of men' (Mark 1.17 par.)?

The disciples derived their vocation to follow Jesus from this combination of a mysterious personal authority and unequalled talent. Who exactly the person was who was calling them and training them to follow him, is a question that was raised only on the initiative of Jesus (Mark 8.27–30 par.), and only exceptionally. What mattered was the correct interpretation of the mission with which the Master was charged. It was wrong to believe that he was sent to call the righteous, or to bring peace upon earth, or to destroy the law, or to concern himself with the Gentiles. His mission was to call sinners, to preach, to serve, to put fire or division between men, and to suffer. The texts about the mission of Jesus are numerous. Moreover, some of them draw a parallel between his mission and that of the disciples (Mark 9.37; Matt. 10.40; Luke 10.16), which shows how much they regarded Jesus as a man to whom a task had been committed, and not as the object of abstract definitions.

Just as they knew that they had been called to their own task by Jesus, they attributed his vocation to 'him who sent him'. In their eyes, Jesus was the object of a special calling by God, seen on the same pattern as that which they received from him. But the dominical sayings are very reticent about the relationship between God and Jesus established by this calling. The terms Father and Son are not limited to the relationship between them, for God is the Father of men (Matt. 5.45–48; 6.8f., 15; etc.). Yet Jesus is the Son in a unique sense (Mark 13.32 par.; cf. Mark 1.11 par.; 9.7 par.), and one saying gives an extremely interesting explanation of the meaning of the term. This is Matt. 11.25–27, quoted on pp. 31f. above. There has been less readiness to treat this as Hellenistic in origin since the discovery of the Qumran hymns, which are full of partial parallels to the text.

Whole books have been written about this saying, which is a good deal different from the other dominical sayings in the synoptic gospels. We shall do no more than emphasize that the idea of revelation is the fundamental one here. If the Son has received full powers from the Father (v. 27a), it is for the purpose of this becoming the exclusive vehicle of the knowledge of the Father (v. 27c). He carries out this function in a way which remains a mystery to everyone (v. 27b), and offers no revelation about himself. To use rather different words, this means that

Jesus has received from God a unique teaching mission to the humble, and that his person is of little significance in the matter. Here we return to the familiar portrait of the man of Nazareth freely chosen by God to bring an eschatological message to men.

This message is set out in Mark 1.15. The authenticity of the terms used here is of only relative importance. There is general agreement that it gives a satisfactory summary of the very varied and sometimes extremely allusive formulae which express the content of the gospel in other texts of the same group. This message falls into two parts: a twofold affirmation concerning divine intervention in human history, and a twofold appeal linked to the previous affirmation by the term 'gospel'.

The action of God is presented in a rather indirect fashion, without the person of God being the subject of the two verbs used. This corresponds to the style of the tradition of the dominical sayings (e.g. Mark 4.25 par.; Luke 14.11, 47f.; Matt. 7.1–5 par.; 7.7–11 par.; the Beatitudes; etc.). The two aspects of the divine intervention remain something of a mystery. The coming to an end of the favourable moment, if this is how the expression *peplērōtai ho kairos* is to be understood, probably signifies the end of the period of grace which the ministry of John the Baptist had been, and the beginning of the much more critical period of the end (cf. Mark 1.7f. par.; Matt. 3.7–10 par.; 11.2–19 par.; 11.20–24 par.; etc.). As for the coming of the kingdom of God, it is an expression which calls to mind numerous metaphors and parables, but also a large number of dominical sayings concerning entry into the kingdom (Mark 9.47; 10.15, 23–25 par.; etc.), the coming of the kingdom (Luke 11.19 par.; 17.20; etc), its imminence (Luke 17.21, if *entos hūmōn* can be taken to mean 'within your grasp'), its possession by some people (Matt. 11.12 par.; Mark 10.14 par.; etc.), and the welcome it is given (Mark 10.15 par.). To all appearances, Jesus asked the disciples to give a considerable place in their teaching to this theme of the kingdom of God, and they saw in it the heart of their master's preaching. The tension between the idea of the kingdom to come and the kingdom which is becoming present is not suppressed anywhere, for whenever the present reality of the kingdom is proclaimed most forcibly, the preaching expresses surprise at seeing the future penetrating the present, and makes it the motivation of an appeal (e.g. Matt. 11.11–15).

The result is not very clear on the conceptual plane, and it is easy to see why interminable debates have arisen and theologians have differed about whether the kingdom of God according to the gospels is a present or a future kingdom. Jesus may have had a clear conception of the kingdom of God. But one must admit that the disciples grasped it only in a confused fashion with the aid of the dominical sayings, and that consequently the reconstruction of Jesus' thought is a hazardous enterprise. Since the parables are no more clear on the subject we go so far as to say that here again it is useless to go beyond the image which the disciples had of Jesus: he was the inspired prophet of a future kingdom of God which, by the will of God, was invading the present and transforming the human condition there and then.

This upheaval, so difficult to conceive of, made the second aspect of Jesus' message indispensable. Mark 1.15 sums it up as a call to conversion and a faith, the object of which is the 'gospel'. It is not necessary to demonstrate here the place of *metanoia* (conversion or repentance) in the dominical sayings. It is a major theme in the teaching of John the Baptist, and Jesus took it up in his turn, then calling upon his disciples to do the same (Mark 6.12 actually reduces their message to this). All the warnings, all the appeals and all the threats in the dominical sayings are variations on this theme of the radical change which man must accept in order to be ready for the coming of the kingdom. 'He who has ears to hear, let him hear' (Matt. 11.15; 13.9 par.; 13.43; 25.29; Mark 7.16; Luke 12.21; 14.35; 21.4). This change cannot be the response to a demonstration or the conclusion of a long period of reflection. It must be the immediate and total reaction to the call to repentance, and its sole justification is the 'gospel'. The coming of the kingdom is visible only in the signs which faith alone can perceive (Matt. 11.2ff. par.; Mark 8.11f. par.; Luke 17.20f.; etc.). Without faith, no one can understand what is happening and realize that Good News is being proclaimed, causing an upheaval in his own situation in an apparently static world. This faith is a certain assurance of the power of God, but is also trust in the bearer of the gospel, whether the Master or his disciples, and the recognition of his authority. It is a long way from the impressive profundity of the faith which Paul describes, and here again one may ask whether Jesus did not go much further in his personal thinking. The disciples who handed on the tradition of the dominical sayings tell us only of a preacher of repentance who calls for unlimited trust in a bold message.

This trust is not solely in the 'gospel', because it has to manifest itself after conversion by 'following Jesus', an idea which the three synoptic writers do not interpret in exactly the same way. Mark regards it as missionary activity, an itinerant life and the acceptance of martyrdom (8.34ff.), while Matthew (16.24ff.) and Luke (9.23ff.) take the expression in a more metaphorical sense, and see it as obedience to the divine will as Jesus has revealed it. One may well hesitate to say which is the oldest meaning. What matters, however, is that Jesus is thought of here as a model as well as a teacher, and more as a leader at the head of his followers than as an example on which one may meditate. In fact, the disciples, in handing down the dominical sayings, show that there is a kind of identity between Jesus and those who became his companions, an inclusion of the latter – in a metaphorical sense at least – in the fate of their Master, which itself formed part of the great drama of the approach of the kingdom of God (cf. for example Matt. 10.32f. par.; 18.20; Mark 3.35 par.; 8.38 par.; 10.38f. par.; 10.42–45 par.; Luke 6.22f. par.). It is doubtful whether all the sayings which contain these ideas originated after the resurrection. The theme of Jesus as the leader to be followed also forms part of the impression produced by the Master upon his disciples, with a certain gloomy element in it.

Some critics, especially those who follow T. W. Manson,[4] consider that this is the very theme which underlies the use of the expression 'Son of man'. In their view, this mysterious figure is a synthesis of the Old Testament ideas of the remnant (Isaiah), of the Servant of the Lord (Deutero-Isaiah), of the 'I' of the Psalms and the Son of man of Daniel 7, all of which designate the people of God that has at last become loyal to its king. The application of the title Son of man to Jesus in numerous passages in the gospels is claimed to be a result of the decision taken by the Master, disappointed by the poor response to his appeals, to take himself the place of the entire holy remnant and to obey unreservedly God's will for his people: that is, to pass through suffering to attain glory.

This thesis has two weak points, which have given rise to serious criticism. First of all, it ignores the existence of a Jewish apocalyptic tradition, illustrated by the First Book of Enoch in the section called 'The Parables', by the Testament of Abraham and by IV Esdras, in which 'the Son of man' is an angelic figure. Its second weakness, which in our opinion is a more serious one, is that it reconstructs the internal development of Jesus in a totally arbitrary way. In our view, the necessity of seeking information of this kind in the texts, which are not capable of giving it, condemns any theory which has recourse to the 'messianic consciousness' of Jesus, and in particular the theory which we have just described. Our documents are not lengthy enough, their derivation from Jesus is not sufficiently direct, and their literary form is not close enough to that of the personal confession for us to go as far as this.

The objection derived from the apocalyptic significance of the expression 'Son of man' is less serious. The phrase 'Son of man' is used in other ways in Hebrew and Aramaic, as can clearly be seen in the Psalms and in the Book of Ezekiel. This may explain certain texts in the gospels such as Mark 2.10 and 2.28 (par.), and is a reminder that the formula is somewhat flexible in nature. The use which the synoptic tradition makes of Daniel 7 permits the critic to say that the Son of man in this tradition may in certain cases represent the people of God, as he does in Daniel. The link between the Son of man and the favourable judgment which will be passed upon the elect at the last day can be very naturally explained in this way (cf. in particular Mark 8.38 par.). As for the identification of the Son of man with the suffering and risen Jesus (Mark 8.31 par.; 9.9–12; 9.31 par; 10.32–34 par.), this is remarkable in itself, and causes no more difficulty to Manson's theory than to any other. In fact it causes less difficulty in his theory, because the 'I' of the Psalms and the Servant of the Lord are figures of suffering.

But the endless debate which continues on this problem indicates that here, even more than in the case of the doctrine of the kingdom of God, the disciples have handed down to use only an

45

image of Jesus, and not a fully worked-out doctrine which might be attributable to their Master, or within which it might be possible to distinguish the authentic elements. Behind the admitted inconsistencies between the various types of dominical sayings which mention the Son of man, can we discern a relatively clear portrait? There is at least one striking fact which has often been pointed out, that only Jesus uses this expression. This means that the tradition does not regard it as a christological confession, like the title 'Christ', for otherwise it would appear in the mouths of the disciples or some other person with whom Jesus speaks. A second striking fact is the constant link which, in the Gospel of Mark at least, exists between the sayings which mention the Son of man and the complex Old Testament background. Daniel 7 is unquestionably present behind the passages mentioning the coming of the Son of man at the end (Mark 8.38; 13.26; 14.62). Behind the passages which speak of the authority of the Son of man upon earth (Mark 2.10; 2.28) lie Genesis 1.27 and 2.15, where man is made the representative of God upon earth. Finally, behind those which present the Son of man as suffering (Mark 9.12; 14.21), there lies a single text which can hardly be other than the servant song in Isaiah 53 (cf. also Mark 8.31; 9.31; 10.32–34).

The portrait of Jesus which emerges from these findings is that of an interpreter of scripture whose general method is to emphasize everywhere the role of man, no doubt along the lines of Psalm 8 (J. Bowker). Thus we are faced once again with the exceptional authority of the Master who, as we said above, feels justified in placing upon the scripture a meaning hitherto imperfectly perceived, and not only upon the law, but also upon other elements in the sacred books: the role of man in the world; the fact that on the last day it is man who will judge his fellows (cf. I Cor. 6.2); the idea painfully acquired by Israel that human suffering is the way to glory. Did Jesus make use of speculations about the primordial man to justify this kind of exegesis (J. Héring)? We shall never know, but there is nothing impossible in this.

What is obvious is that the disciples were struck by what their Master taught them on this matter, and asked themselves whether he who spoke to them in this way was not himself the man whose role he described in such impressive terms. This led them to wonder about the person of Jesus, over and above his mission. In this way they prepared the way for such developments as the assimilation by the evangelist Mark of Jesus' commentary on Isaiah 53 to a prophecy of the Passion (8.31; 9.31; 10.32–34). But the tradition itself seems to have remained cautious, and to have been very discreet in introducing into the dominical sayings the statement that Jesus and the Son of man were identical. This is a field in which the disciples gathered together the allusions made by their Master, but did not allow themselves to go beyond this.

Thus the portrait of Jesus which emerges from the dominical sayings handed down by the disciples and gathered together in the synoptic gospels lacks any messianic features in the strict sense, and does not include any christological title for the Master. On the other hand, it reveals him to have been a personality endowed with extraordinary talent and authority, to whom God had committed the eschatological mission to Israel in the fullest sense: that of bringing the kingdom of God to Israel by making the nation understand that the Master was offering it the authentic interpretation of the divine will and revelation, together with the possibility of appropriating it by conversion and faith. This portrait also shows him to us as the founder of a group of healing preachers who helped and accompanied the Master in carrying out his task. Finally, it gives an important place to the themes of the renunciation of all human security, of the opposition Jesus met, of the suffering he undertook and of the love of one's enemies: it describes a conqueror, but a conqueror whose triumph owes nothing to compromise nor to physical violence, and everything to the certainty of the action of God which nothing in the end can withstand.

4

The Jesus of the 'Apophthegms'

Rudolf Bultmann borrowed the term 'apophthegm' from the history of Greek literature to describe the brief anecdotes in the synoptic tradition which centre upon a saying of Jesus, and in which the narrative has no other purpose than to provide a framework for this saying. He divides the apophthegms into two main categories: conflict and didactic sayings on the one hand, and biographical apophthegms on the other. We shall use this classification, because it corresponds well with the factors of form and content which characterize these various stories.

What portrait of Jesus do these texts reveal amongst those who handed them on? There is an obvious relationship between the apophthegms and the dominical sayings, because in both the central point is a saying of Jesus. Thus we might expect to find here a portrait of the Master very similar to that which we described in the previous chapter. At the same time, if we were to detect a difference in the agents of transmission between the apophthegms and the dominical sayings, this might give a certain substance to the nuances distinguishing the portraits of Jesus which correspond to each.

The 'biographical apophthegms' are often so close to being dominical sayings with a few words of introduction that some of them have already been used from time to time in Chapter 3. Since they are not excessive in number, the list given in Bultmann, *The History of the Synoptic Tradition* can be reproduced here:[1]

Mark 1.16–20 par.; 2.14 par.: Calling of disciples.
Luke 9.57–62 and Matt. 8.19–22: Following Jesus.
Mark 3.2–21, 31–35 par.: The true kinsmen.

Luke 11.27f.: The blessing of Mary.

Mark 6.1–6 par.: The rejection in the home village.

Mark 10.13–16 par.: Jesus blesses the children.

Mark 12.41–44 par.: The widow's mite.

Luke 10.38–42: Mary and Martha.

Luke 17.11–19: The healing of the ten lepers.

Luke 19.1–10: Zacchaeus.

Luke 19.39f. and Matt. 21.15f.: The praise of the disciples (Matt.: children).

Matt. 17.24–27: The Temple tax.

Luke 13.31–33: Jesus and Herod.

Mark 11.15–19 par.: The cleansing of the Temple.

Mark 13.1f. par.: The prophecy of the destruction of the Temple.

Luke 19.41–44: The prophecy of the destruction of Jerusalem.

Mark 14.3–9 par.: The anointing in Bethany.

Luke 23.27–31: The ascent to the cross.

In Bultmann's view, these texts should be supplemented by two narratives which are centred upon a saying uttered by an interlocutor of Jesus: the episode of the Syro-Phoenician woman (Mark 7.24–31 par.) and that of the centurion of Capernaum (Matt. 8.5–13 par.). But the first is simply a miracle story with a dialogue. Only the second should be included here.

One may ask with Bultmann whether many of these little anecdotes are not 'ideal scenes' intended to make the saying of Jesus more comprehensible than when it was handed down in isolation. Actually the narrative often lacks detail, and does not have the rhythmical form which would suggest that it had been composed to be memorized. In our view, the composition of such 'ideal scenes' should therefore be located at the time of the redaction of the gospels rather than at the stage of oral transmission. The evangelists might in fact have been tempted to invent a little story to link an isolated saying of Jesus to the narrative context where they wished to place it. There is some possibility that this may be the case in Mark 3.20f. and 3.21–35 par.; 10.13–16 par.; Luke 9.57–62 and Matt. 8.19–22; Luke 19.41–44; Luke 23.27–31.

But we believe that in all other cases the narratives are older than this, and that there is no reason to locate their composition elsewhere than at the starting-point of the oral tradition, as far as most of them are concerned. Since there is no reason for locating this starting-point any later in the case of the apophthegms than in the case of the dominical sayings, the narrative element that the former contain therefore goes back in most cases to the teaching given by Jesus to his disciples, even though it was not intended to be memorized as exactly as the sayings.

That is, the historical probability of these anecdotes is certain in so far as they give a version of the facts corresponding to the point of view of Jesus and his companions. These are, of course, minor events, mostly quite insignificant. We should note, however, the real importance of the expulsion of the money-changers from the Temple, to which we shall return below, pp. 111ff. We should also note the straightforward way in which the apophthegm of the ten lepers (Luke 17.11–19) tells of a healing carried out by God thanks to the faith of the sick person, Jesus being no more than the catalyst. This edifying narrative, accompanied by a word of warning to Israel and typical of rabbinic miracle narratives, is a good example of the way Jesus taught his disciples to use an episode of this kind. Similarly, the healing of the centurion's child gives a fine and dignified interpretation of the miracle granted to faith (Matt. 8.5–13 par.), which one can attribute without hesitation to the teaching given by Jesus to his followers, at least as it was understood by them. We shall see later that not all the gospel miracle stories are of this calibre.

The biographical apophthegms form part of the tradition entrusted by Jesus to his disciples to guide their community life and their missionary activities, in the same way as the dominical sayings. Like the latter, they may have undergone a number of distortions in the course of transmission, or even, in a few cases, have been produced spontaneously in imitation of an already existing apophthegm or an authentic dominical saying. But it is quite impossible to distinguish with certainty between those which are historical and those which are not. As in the case of the dominical sayings, we must resign ourselves to giving up this attempt and consider the whole tradition of biographical apophthegms without claiming to do more than distinguish in them the portrait which the disciples had of Jesus.

This portrait is not as detailed as that of the dominical sayings, which are much more numerous and diverse. It does no more than complement the latter on a number of points. Jesus is seen as the authoritative and demanding Master (Luke 9.57–62 and Matt. 8.19–22), who calls for strict obedience from those who take his part (Mark 3.31–35 par.; cf. Luke 11.27f.) and vigorously advocates an unreserved obedience to the will of God, even in the most mundane matters (Luke 17.14; Matt. 17.24–27; Mark 11.15–19 par.). But he is also presented as the friend of the humble, either of children (Mark 10.13–16 par.; Matt. 21.15f.), of defenceless women (Mark 12.41–44 par.; 14.3–9 par.; Luke 10.38–42; 23.27–31) or men excluded from Jewish society (Luke 17.11–19; 19.1–10). He appears himself as a reprobate (Mark 3.20f., 31–35 par.; 6.1–6 par.; Luke 23.27–31) who deals somewhat brutally with the established authorities (Luke 13.31–33; Mark 11.15–19 par.).

But to a special degree he is represented in the guise of a prophet, which explains his acts of authority. He proclaims salvation to those to whom it is granted (Mark 10.14; Luke 17.19; 19.9f.; Mark 14.6–9 par.); and also disaster to those who are condemned to perdition (Mark 13.1f. par.; Luke 19.41–44; 23.27–31). His words are clearly regarded as efficacious, like those of the Old Testament prophets. This Master and prophet displays no messianic features in the strict sense, in spite of his extraordinary authority.

The conflict dialogues conducted by Jesus with various adversaries, and his debates with supporters or friends, form a much larger group of traditions. They too centre upon a saying of Jesus which usually concludes a narrative. The narrative is very brief and has no other purpose except to lead up to the statement with which Jesus demonstrates his superiority over his adversaries or his disciples.

The list given by Bultmann[2] falls into four parts:

1. The conflict is occasioned by Jesus' healings:
Mark 3.1–6 par.: The sabbath healing of the man with the withered hand.

Luke 14.1–6: The sabbath healing of the man with the dropsy.

Luke 13.10–17: The sabbath healing of the crippled woman.

Mark 3.22–30 par.: The dispute about exorcism.

Mark 2.1–12 par.: The healing of the paralytic.

2. The conflict is otherwise occasioned by the conduct of Jesus or the disciples:

Mark 2.23–28 par.: Plucking corn on the sabbath.

Mark 7.1–23 par.: The dispute about 'clean' and 'unclean'.

Mark 2.15–17 par.: Eating with publicans and sinners.

Mark 2.18–22 par.: The question of fasting.

Mark 11.27–33 par.: The question of authority.

Luke 7.36–50: The sinner and the feast.

3. The Master is questioned (by the disciples or others):

Mark 10.17–31 par.: The rich young man.

Mark 12.28–34 par.: The chief commandment.

Luke 12.13f.: The dispute over inheritance.

Luke 13.1–5: The slaughter of the Galilaeans.

Matt. 11.2–19 par.: John the Baptist's question.

Mark 10.35–45 par.: The question of the sons of Zebedee.

Mark 9.38–40 par.: The rival exorcist.

Luke 17.20f.: The coming of the kingdom of God.

Mark 11.20–25 par.: The cursed fig tree.

Luke 9.51–56: The inhospitable Samaritans.

4. Questions asked by opponents:

Mark 12.13–17: Tribute to Caesar.

Mark 12.18–27 par.: The Sadducees.

Mark 10.2–12: Divorce.

Useful though it is, this classification overlooks an important fact: the conflict narratives are grouped in Mark in a very striking way. In fact they are almost all gathered in two relatively long collections (2.1 to 3.6, and 11.27–33, with 12.13–34) and in two shorter collections (3.22–30 and 7.1–23), each of which refers to one or two set themes. These collections are no doubt in essence the work of Mark, but one of them at least probably existed already at the stage of the oral tradition, which here as well as elsewhere made an effort at systematization.

The collection which goes back to the oral tradition is in our view that in Mark 11 and 12, where we see Jesus routing the various leading groups of Palestinian Judaism in turn: 'The chief priests and the scribes and the elders', which certainly refers to the members of the Jerusalem Sanhedrin (11.27–33), who are the object of an additional attack in Mark 12.1–12; the Pharisees and the Herodians (12.13–27); the Sadducees (12.18–27); and the scribes (12.28–34), whose representative seems ready to be persuaded by the obvious superiority of Jesus. Apart from this sociological pattern, which faithfully reflects the reality of Palestine, there is a great similarity of structure between the four narratives in question (Mark 12.1–12, a Marcan addition which we shall discuss again below, p. 88, may be neglected here): the provocative question of the adversaries immediately following their identification; a counter-attack by Jesus who skilfully avoids the trap and has the last word; Jesus' adversaries vanish.

This collection gives a portrait of Jesus which is not absolutely in accord with that which emerges from the other conflict dialogues and didactic dialogues. Here Jesus appears as a subtle and skilful debater, who will not allow himself to be caught in the trap of rabbinic discussion, but places himself on the same ground as his adversaries, the Jewish intellectuals of the time. The dominant note in this collection is the Master's skill, which was displayed each time before the best trained minds of his people, in spite of his no doubt scanty education. Since this collection may perfectly well go back to the origin of the oral tradition, the portrait of Jesus which it presents must correspond to the impression he made upon his disciples: that of a simple man like themselves who could impose his law upon the finest minds. They drew from this both an example and a support in their own contacts with these people.

The other conflict dialogues seem to have been handed down in isolation in the tradition, either singly or in pairs. It will be noted that the Gospel of Matthew remains content to reproduce those supplied by the Gospel of Mark, without adding to them, while the Gospel of Luke adds to those derived from Mark four other anecdotes of this kind (Luke 7.36–50; 13.10–17; 14.1–6; 17.20f.), but sums up in a radical fashion the debate on the clean and the unclean, which it regards as out of

53

date (Luke 11.37–41). On the other hand, in certain of the dialogues borrowed from Mark, the Gospel of Matthew tones down the more provocative features of the declarations or the behaviour of Jesus: Mark 2.27 is omitted in Matthew, as in Luke, in order to tone down somewhat the attack on the sabbath rest; in the case of the man with the withered hand, in Matt. 12.9–14 the conflict is provoked by a trick question posed by the adversaries and not by an initiative of Jesus, as in Mark. In Matt. 15.1–9 a clever inversion makes Jesus' denunciation of the 'tradition of the elders' less arbitrary than in Mark 7.1–8; in Matt. 22.34–46, the fusion of the debate on the greatest commandment and the saying concerning the attribution to the Messiah of the title 'Son of David' renders the latter less unexpected and abrupt than in Mark 12.35–37.

All these changes suggest that the evangelist Matthew, although inclined to denounce the sins of the scribes and Pharisees, was embarrassed by the aggressiveness attributed to Jesus in certain of the controversy dialogues which he read in Mark, and by those which he may have known elsewhere in the tradition and which Luke reproduced. In fact there is in these dialogues a bitter tone which has no equivalent in the collection in Mark 11 and 12 (and par.). Jesus is presented in them as a ferocious denouncer of the sins and pretensions of the Jewish leaders of the time. He provokes conflicts, adopts an aggressive attitude for no immediate reason, and uses the language of an angry prophet and no longer that of a skilled debater.

Some critics regard these two approaches as deriving from two different periods in the ministry of Jesus, but the difficulty of undertaking reconstructions of this kind is well known. Moreover, according to the synoptic gospels, the least aggressive controversies are those which occur only shortly before the passion, while one would expect the contrary to be the case. Ought we then to follow L. Cerfaux in attributing the preservation of all the conflict dialogues, moulded during the very first years by the Jerusalem community, to the churches of Antioch, Caesarea, and Damascus, and not to that of Jerusalem, which had been re-Judaized by James?[3] The hypothesis is an interesting one, but in our view needs some correction. We consider first of all that the transmission of the conflict dialogues of Mark 11 and 12 must be located at Jerusalem. As

54

for the others, we believe (like Cerfaux) that their origin must be located as far back as that of those in Mark 11 and 12. Since the distinction between the authentic and the inauthentic is no more feasible here than for any other passages, we shall avoid a detailed analysis of the content of each conflict dialogue with the aim of pronouncing upon its origin. But it is very likely that the transmission of the dialogues which were not preserved at Jerusalem took place in a church context, with the aim of serving the needs of Christian apologetic. The churches proposed by Cerfaux are certainly likely, especially if one considers the links which connected Caesarea and Antioch to the group of 'Hellenists' in the book of Acts (Acts 8.40; 11.19ff.; 21.3ff.), with its extreme tendencies.

Thus one can allow that a common portrait of Jesus underlies all these controversy narratives, that of a skilled and vigorous Master who was not afraid to confront the best debaters of contemporary Judaism, and knew how to use these discussions to impose not his own interpretation of the tradition, but a completely unparalleled personal authority. Thereafter, the different settings in which they were handed down varied the portrait slightly. Jesus is more subtle in the Jerusalem narratives, and more aggressive in other dialogues of this kind.

Can one trace a particular portrait of Jesus behind the *didactic dialogues* of the synoptic tradition, which, following Bultmann, we have listed together with the conflict dialogues (the third group above, p. 52)? The small group of ten passages – excluding parallels – to which this term can be applied provides a rather narrow basis for such an enquiry. There is little risk of error in saying that these anecdotes were handed down in the same circumstances as the dominical sayings, and that the portrait of Jesus reflected in them is bound to resemble very closely that which we saw underlying the dominical sayings (cf. above, p. 48).

However, the portrait already described is supplemented here by a number of special features. The most frequent, which forms the kernel of several of these dialogues, is the firmness with which Jesus refuses to play the roles or to say the things that people try to impose upon him. He is willing neither to be deceived by the flatteries of the rich man (Mark 10.17f.), nor to act as a judge concerning inheritances (Luke 12.13f.), nor as the protector of the sons of Zebedee (Mark 10.35ff.), nor as the manipulator of fire from heaven (Luke 9.51–56). He will not be drawn into saying that the Galileans massacred by Pilate were sinners (Mark 9.38–40), or when the kingdom of God is to come (Luke 17.20f.). In short, the Master whom the disciples knew could not be imposed upon. Not that he refuses everything; far from it, as we shall see. But there are limits beyond which he will not go, and accommodations which he will not make.

Another frequent feature in these didactic dialogues is the way in which Jesus draws his interlocutors into the argument in the most personal way, when they believe that they can obtain instruction from him without being really involved. The rich man is called to dispose of all his riches (Mark 10.21); the sons of Zebedee are required to think of martyrdom and the service of others, not of heavenly reward (Mark 10.35ff.); the disciples, preoccupied with supernatural botany, find themselves exhorted to pray (Mark 11.21–25); those who recount catastrophes are encouraged to repent (Luke 13.1–5); the Pharisees, preoccupied with complicated apocalyptic calculations, are suddenly faced with a kingdom which is within their grasp (Luke 17.20f.). All these examples show the same attitude on the part of Jesus. Once again it is the personal authority of the Master which is seized and preserved, a quite fierce authority which will not accept any half measures and which calls anyone who tries to make use of it to change his conduct radically.

Finally, there is a third feature in the portrait of Jesus which we find in the didactic dialogues: Jesus' capacity to derive exceedingly bold teaching from an insignificant episode. This is true of the reply to the question of John the Baptist (Matt. 11.2ff. par.), which completely immerses the hearers in the eschatological crisis and endeavours to relate this crisis to the whole history of salvation; of the reply to the Pharisees (Luke 17.20f.), which totally transforms current conceptions of the coming of the kingdom of God; of the teaching on the efficaciousness of prayer which follows the episode of the cursed fig tree (Mark 11.21–25), and which assumes that supernatural power is committed to the disciples, obviously in connection with their mission of proclaiming the kingdom. Here again we find the Master who uses paradoxical and striking phrases, as we learnt to know him in the dominical sayings.

In short, the Jesus whom we meet in the apophthegms is the same on the whole as we find in the dominical sayings, for the simple reason that the latter give us the impression which Jesus produced upon his disciples, as was the case for the sayings. The most important variation comes from the fact that many of the conflict dialogues were transmitted in the rather special church setting which had long been influenced by the Hellenists, and which thus took on a more forceful colouring than those for which the church of Jerusalem was responsible.

5

The Jesus of the Biographical Narratives

I have already explained (above, p. 26) why we shall study here neither the infancy narratives nor the narratives of the resurrection appearances, which can both be regarded as comparatively late legends of virtually no biographical interest. I shall discuss the miracle stories below, pp. 97ff. Both their origin and transmission pose very special problems. We must now consider two categories of narrative which differ profoundly from one another: the scattered narratives which are found in that part of the synoptic gospels which precedes the passion; and the four gospel narratives of the passion, to which must be added the discovery of the empty tomb (Mark 16.1–8 par.), which forms its conclusion.

The scattered narratives found in the synoptics between the infancy narratives and those of the passion include in the first instance various passages concerning John the Baptist: the activity of the Baptist (Mark 1.1–3; Matt. 3.1–12; Luke 3.1–18) and his martyrdom (Mark 6.17–29 par.). We shall not analyse them, however interesting this might prove to be. They do not in fact give us any direct information about Jesus.

On the other hand, the narrative of the baptism of Jesus by John the Baptist (Mark 1.9–11 par.); that of the temptation of Jesus (Mark 1.12f.; Matt. 4.1–11; Luke 4.1–12); the confession of Peter at Caesarea Philippi (Mark 8.27–30 par.); the transfiguration (Mark 9.2–8 par.); the solemn entry of Jesus into Jerusalem (Mark 11.1–10 par.) must be taken into account. Perhaps some of the narratives peculiar to the Fourth Gospel, such as those of the calling of the disciples (John 1.35–51), the conversion of the Samaritans (John 4.4–42) or the request of the Greeks to see Jesus (John 12.20ff.), should also be included. These latter ought rather to be described as biographical apophthegms, for in them Jesus utters, more or less at length, sayings which can be said to be the sole justification of the narratives. But the part of these narratives which derives from oral tradition is very small, even in the eyes of C. H. Dodd.[1] The redactional activity of the author of the Fourth Gospel has not left many traces of what existed before he took the narratives over.

If we restrict ourselves to the small number of narratives in the synoptics, have we to regard them as a separate category of oral tradition? We do not think so. The confession of Peter at Caesarea Philippi, as it is recounted in Mark 8.27ff., clearly seems to have been deprived of its conclusion by the evangelist, who tries immediately after the saying of Peter to stress the necessity of suffering, and in order to do so suppresses the congratulations of the Master to the first disciple to acknowledge him. The favourable reply of Jesus, which is lacking in Mark, is found in Matt. 16.17 (the two verses which follow form a separate saying). If this or a similar hypothesis is accepted, the episode is a didactic dialogue or an apophthegm, where the essential kernel is the saying of Jesus. In other words, the emphasis is less upon the confession of Jesus as the Christ, even though this is said to be correct, than upon the revelation received by Peter. This is obviously a tradition meant, from a very early period, to give a particular authority to Peter. In fact little attention is paid to the title of Christ; the other acknowledgments to Jesus are not rejected, but are implicitly characterized as human points of view. At the decisive moment the attention is drawn to the disciple inspired by God, and not to the Master. This lack of interest in the title which the Christian church of the first generation was to place at the centre of its faith encourages us to think that the tradition in question may have been meant to establish the authority of Peter, even during Jesus' lifetime, amongst the healing preachers who were gathered about Jesus.

Thus one can suppose that the titles attributed here to Jesus by 'the people' are those which were given to him even before the crucifixion. However late the didactic dialogue or apophthegm may be thought to be, it is difficult to see how one could have chosen to describe as 'John the Baptist' (resur-rected: cf. Mark 6.14–16) someone who himself had been executed. The same difficulty applies to the title of Elijah: How can a man put to death be regarded as the reincarnation of a prophet whom in his time God preserved from death? Mark 9.11–13 and Matt. 11.14 are puzzled by this difficulty in re-spect of the identification of John the Baptist with Elijah. Identical problems would have arisen if the attempt had been made to make the same identification in the case of Jesus after his execution. By calling Jesus 'prophet', 'John the Baptist' and 'Elijah' the crowd were demonstrating that they saw in him an eschatological messenger from God acting in the same way as the prophets, through the word; and they were also attributing to him the role of the reconciler of all the Israelites, which according to Malachi 4.5f. was that of Elijah *redivivus*.

It is curious and interesting that the reply of the disciples to these pre-paschal titles, a reply also no doubt made before the crucifixion and resurrection, was to describe their Master as Messiah, or, if one prefers the Greek word, as Christ. Thus the conception held by the disciples is not the same as that of the multitude, even though the latter no doubt also applied this title to Jesus at the end of his ministry (cf. below p. 116). As has often been pointed out, the characteristics of the Messiah which were expected at the time were not to be found in the historical Jesus, who was neither a glorious king nor a priest. And Jesus' words of approval to Peter (Matt. 16.17) show that the disciple was making a kind of 'leap of faith' which was not based on objec-tive and verifiable data. In the picture the disciples had of Jesus there was an element of enthusiasm, no doubt based upon the personal authority of Jesus and the eschatological nature of his mission – whether the use of the title 'Messiah' is traced back to some time before the resurrection, as we think it should be, or not. This element cannot be neglected, any more than one can ignore the acceptance of the title by Jesus. Acceptance of it shows that the Master thought that the recognition of the es-chatological character of his mission was important, or at least that the disciples were not aware of any difficulty in applying the title 'Messiah' to the person of him who had drawn his people into an adventure as original as it was impressive, the encounter with the kingdom of God.

There may be some relationship between the primitive form of the confession of Peter and that of the narratives of the baptism of Jesus (Mark 1.9–11 par.) and of the transfiguration (Mark 9.2–8 par.). The resemblance between the latter two is obvious. Both include a setting up of a communication between heaven and earth, and are centred upon words uttered by a heavenly voice which designate Jesus as the 'beloved Son of God'. The similarity is all the more striking since these are the only two occasions in which the voice from on high is heard in the synoptic gospels, which are very reticent on this point. In view of the extreme solemnity of the two declarations by God, it is difficult to see why the relative length of the narrative makes it impossible to include these two passages amongst the apophthegms. We therefore propose to consider them as such, and not as 'legends', as Bultmann does. The mythical feature that these narratives display by no means excludes this, once one realizes that the saying was the principal element about which the narrative crystallized. It may in fact be the case that these two narratives were handed down together in the oral tradition, as is suggested by an admittedly late passage, II Peter 1.17f. In this case, the aim of both would have been to reinforce the authority of the three disciples close to Jesus: Peter, James and John. Just as Jesus heard the voice of God at his baptism, so the disciples received the revelation from on high on the mountain of the transfiguration and learnt in a very special way to obey the Master.

Whether this latter hypothesis is true or not, these two apophthegms include, like the confession of Peter, the attribution of a christological title to Jesus; not 'Messiah' this time, but 'Son of God'. There has been much discussion of the meaning of this expression here. It is frequently found in other religions to describe all kinds of beings. It is clear that the Greek sense of a 'divine being', differing in substance from common mortals, influenced the Christian use of the title even before the end of the first century: the infancy narratives, and particularly that of Luke, confirm this. But it is equally clear that the title 'Son of God', commonly found in the Old Testament, was originally understood by the disciples in the sense that it has there.[2] That is, it was used to designate Jesus as the man to whom God had given an important mission and who obeyed the divine command. Uttered by God himself, it signifies the choosing of the person to whom it is applied, especially as the adjective *agapētos*, 'beloved', which accompanies it in the three synoptic gospels in the narrative of the baptism, and in Mark and Matthew in that of the transfiguration, has a meaning approximating to 'chosen', if one compares its use in the Old Testament, and notes that Luke substitutes the word *eklelegmenos*, 'elect', in his version of the saying at the transfiguration.

These two declarations by the heavenly voice have sometimes been seen as quotations from the Old Testament. In fact there is a certain similarity between the words and those of Isaiah 42.1 and Psalm 2.7 in particular. Thus it is not surprising that Matthew should have transformed the words at the baptism into a literal quotation of Isaiah 42.1, while the witnesses to the 'Western' text make the same words in Luke 3.22 into an exact quotation of Psalm 2.7. But it is not clear why God should quote his own words in order to pronounce on the subject of Jesus. Here we have not the fulfilment of prophecies, but the special revelation which is necessary for the proper understanding of the mission of the prophet of Nazareth. This revelation resembles various passages in the Old Testament, but is not a quotation from them.

Moreover, there is no reason why these narratives, and in particular the words attributed to the heavenly voice, should not be based on mystical experiences on the part of Jesus in the one case and of the three disciples in the other. There are too many indications of Jesus' certainty of being the 'Son of God' in the Jewish sense, beginning with his use in prayer of 'Father' in the familiar form *abba*, for it to be possible to dismiss this idea in his case. And in the case of the disciples there are too many tendencies to visions, beginning with the appearances of the risen Christ, for it to be possible to argue that the episode recounted in the form of the transfiguration narrative is improbable. But it must be admitted that the very reserved language of the oral tradition tells us only what the disciples as a whole retained of these two events. This is no more than that there were exceptional links between their Master and God. Such a conviction may perhaps have led to the use of the term 'Son of God' within the group of the disciples and to that of 'Messiah' in addressing the multitude, which was more accustomed to this title. In any case, the Messianic image of Jesus put forward here is not the classical one, as it is identical neither with Essene Messianism, nor that of the Pharisees, nor that of the Zealots.

The tradition concerning the temptation of Jesus reveals the same idea (Mark 1.12f.; Matt. 4.1–11; Luke 4.1–12). This tradition, which Mark merely summarizes in an almost incomprehensible way for the sake of brevity, gives every appearance of being a *midrash* on a number of Old Testament texts (Deut. 8.3; Psalm 91.1ff.; Deut. 6.16; 6.13) or a conflict dialogue in which the role of the adversary is played by Satan. It perhaps gives us an echo of the exegesis practised by Jesus, and in any case conveys the impression which the disciples felt of the difficulty of defining the role of Jesus in classical terms. Jesus is neither a magician carrying out miracles for his own benefit, even in a case of urgent need; nor a fanatic seeking to impress the people by forcing the hand of God to bring about supernatural interventions on his behalf; nor a political Messiah who would have taken a dangerous short cut towards world power by submitting to Satan. The episode gives us nothing more than this threefold negative definition, which no doubt reflects accusations made against Jesus during his lifetime or shortly after the crucifixion. The mission of Jesus is a new phenomenon which traditional expressions cannot adequately describe; and this is how the disciples saw it.

The account of the entry of Jesus into Jerusalem (Mark 11.1–10 par.) contains legendary elements (vv. 2–6) which have a striking resemblance to the episode of the preparation for the Passover in Mark 14.13–16 par. One may well ask whether these five verses may not have been borrowed by the author of the Gospel of Mark from this other narrative, in order to make more impressive the somewhat modest scene which existed in the tradition, of the Master's entry into Jerusalem riding a donkey, and accompanied by a group of enthusiastic pilgrims. The rest of the narrative, with the kind of antiphonal chant which concludes it, gives the impression of being a sort of liturgy representing the arrival of the Master amongst his followers, and prefiguring the Parousia. We shall see below (p. 111) how its existence may be explained.

Thus a study of the biographical narratives which do not belong to the Passion narrative shows that they do not form a

63

separate tradition, but can all be placed in other categories: apophthegms, conflict dialogues and didactic dialogues, together with liturgical traditions amplified by considerable borrowings from the Passion narrative. We must now briefly show why the Passion narrative must be regarded as a cultic document, before it is possible to recover the portrait of Jesus conceived by those amongst whom this narrative was formed.

All critics agree that the topographical and chronological framework of the Passion narrative as we find it in the four gospels is much more coherent, much fuller and much older than that of the rest of the gospels, which is the product of the redactional activity of the evangelists. Instead of the vagueness found elsewhere, we have here a series of episodes following in rapid succession at a date, time and place which are precisely stated. The somewhat hasty conclusion is sometimes drawn from this that these narratives are historical in their entirety. In fact the difficulties raised by the four gospel narratives of the Passion are numerous. One has only to recall the serious chronological disagreement between John, where Jesus dies on 14 Nisan, the eve of the Passover, and the synoptics, which place the crucifixion on the 15th; the improbable accumulation of the events between the Last Supper and the crucifixion according to Mark; the extraordinary legal confusion represented by the double trial of Jesus as recorded in Mark and Matthew; the remarkable role played in the narratives by allusions to scripture, which have led some scholars to say that we have here a kind of midrashic legend, the key to which is an exegetical and not an historical one; and so one might go on.

In fact, between our texts and the reality of history there lies the thick screen of the redactional activity of the evangelists and the equally thick screen of the history of the oral tradition. Once more, we have access to the interpretation of events by the disciples of Jesus, rather than to these events themselves. We believe that the intervention of the evangelists at the moment of redaction was not as great in the case of this narrative as with the rest of the gospels, precisely because of the firmer framework which retained each episode in its place. Thus Matthew permits himself no more than a few additions to the Passion as Mark recounts it (Matt. 26.21, 52–54; 27.3–10, 19, 24f., 43, 51–53, 62–66) and a few even more limited suppressions (Matthew has no equivalent to Mark 14.51f.; 15.44), while he takes many more liberties in the rest of his book. The much more serious differences between Mark and Luke are due to the fact that Luke is following another source here. As for John, he certainly made many more changes than the other evangelists in the redaction of his Passion narrative; nevertheless, he respected the main outlines of the tradition which he used, as is revealed by the unusual resemblance that can be seen in this case between his narrative and that of the synoptics.

Taking into account this prudence on the part of the evangelists, critics often explain the differences between their narratives of the Passion by the use of different sources. We believe that while Matthew used Mark and virtually nothing else, Luke reproduced a Passion narrative somewhat different from Mark's source, and made little or no use of the latter. As for John, we believe that he was inspired solely by a different Passion narrative. With the majority of those who accept that there were several traditional narratives, we also believe that they all go back to one archetype, very close to the events which it recounts. But what did this archetype of the Passion narrative contain and why was it produced?

Many scholars would reply to the first of these questions that it formed no more than the skeleton of the present narrative, giving a very brief account of the arrest, the double condemnation, the journey to the cross, the crucifixion and the death of Jesus. In particular, this thesis is held by R. Bultmann, followed by scholars who differ from him as much as J. Jeremias[3] or Vincent Taylor.[4] Bultmann sets out his thesis in *The History of the Synoptic Tradition*.[5] We are not ourselves convinced that the few obvious joins and other anomalies which can be detected in Mark's account are a sufficient reason for dismembering a narrative which in other respects is so coherent. Of course there are questions to be asked about the presence in the Passion narrative of the story of Jesus' last meal, or of the episode of the empty tomb. But the other breaches of continuity which can be detected here and there are problems for the historian rather than for the literary critic: they do not cast doubt on the coherence of the narrative, but on the historical probability of particular details. One example is the Gethsemane episode; it cannot be shown to be a late insertion by the arbitrary affirmation that Mark 14.43–52 originally followed 14.27–31, that the pericope formed by verses 32–41a was originally isolated and only became joined to the rest by virtue of the addition of vv. 33f. and 41b–42 by the evangelists, and that vv. 36 and 38 are also additions. This scene, which records the words of a prayer of Jesus which no one heard, raises many *historical* difficulties, but there is no serious reason for excluding it from the primitive *narrative* of the Passion. It does not interrupt any sequence of events, is not in conflict with the tone of the narrative, and, even if it shows some evidence of slight alteration (the double version of the prayer in vv. 35 and 36?), should not be excluded from the primitive tradition for this reason. Another example of the danger of the application of literary criticism in the narrower sense of the word is the way in which Bultmann states that the narrative of Jesus' appearance before the Sanhedrin is no more than a late development of the phrase in Mark 15.1 par. Although he denies it,[6] the historical difficulty of this scene is the principal reason for his hypothesis, which otherwise rests only on a few internal incoherencies in Mark 14.55–64 par. At most, these suggest the presence of a later addition to an already existing narrative (vv. 57–59).

It is not necessary to multiply examples. We believe that those we have given are sufficient to show that the search for a very short primitive Passion narrative leads criticism along a false trail, and confuses literary and historical considerations in an unfortunate fashion. In our view, the problem should be approached differently, ignoring entirely, in the first instance, the historical problem of the trial and the death of Jesus. Can one think of a setting where the formation of so long and coherent a narrative as that of the Passion could have been produced in order to satisfy practical needs? It is undoubtedly necessary to look for a church setting where Christians meditated upon the unjust and redeeming death of the Master, rather than attempted to establish facts with a legal or apologetic purpose in mind. This collective meditation could hardly be other than cultic in nature, and must have originated at Jerusalem, no doubt at the very moment when the disciples began their life as a community in that city. With its detailed chronological framework, which in places is even very close to the pattern of Jewish prayer times (cf. Mark 15.1, 25, 33, 34,

66

47, with its succession of events taking place every three hours), the narrative suggests a liturgical evocation of the martyrdom of Jesus, in which the times when the liturgy took place were more important than the chronology of the events themselves.

Thus in our view the solution of the literary problem of the Passion narrative is to be sought in the direction suggested by the Canadian Philip Carrington[7] and the German scholar Gottfried Schille.[8] Both see in this narrative the text of a liturgy of the Christian Passover celebrated at Jerusalem from the very earliest times. One may add with Schille that this liturgy was probably celebrated in the very places which the tradition associated with the various stages in Jesus' martyrdom, or at least in the neighbourhood of those places, which were sometime inaccessible. In fact, without going into the details of the two hypotheses we have quoted, we may say that there is no question that a kind of Christian pilgrimage to Jerusalem was superimposed upon the Jewish pilgrimage, in which the members of Christian churches which were largely Jewish would normally participate: cf. the journeys which Paul made to Jerusalem *on the occasion of Jewish festivals* (Acts 18.20–22; 20.16).

We do not propose here to undertake the enormous and impossible task of reconstructing the oldest form of this pilgrim's missal. The essential thing is that the 'guide' was not very different from the versions which later served as sources for Mark, Luke and John. To take up a comparison proposed by Carrington, this primitive narrative would have been the 'roll' read at the Christian Passover, just as the Book of Esther was that which was read at the Jewish feast of Purim, no doubt from its origin. The two documents are not very different in size, and the comparison is interesting, even if the narrative of the Passion remained in oral form until it spread outside Jerusalem, at which point it became separated from the liturgy which had given rise to it. Here again, we are concerned with the portrait of Jesus found in it. What did the believers who instituted this pilgrimage and those who took part in it think of their Master?

It may be objected that this post-resurrection representation of the person of the crucified Christ has no great bearing on the history of the man Jesus. This brings us to the central problem raised for the biographer of Jesus by the gospel narratives of the Passion. Has faith left any room in them for facts that history can use? The question has been discussed time and again. The opponents of historicity, who are far from all being convinced that there is absolutely nothing historical behind the narrative, emphasize the impossibility of the legal procedures in the gospel narratives, with their double trial, the haste of the Sanhedrin and the inconsistency of Pilate's behaviour. They criticize the improbability of the Marcan chronology, and point to the fact that it is contradicted by the Fourth Gospel, and to the way Matthew and Luke water it down to make the course of events less incredibly rapid. They rightly stress that some episodes are so packed with allusions to scripture that one may ask whether they were not created by meditation on the Old Testament passages to which they allude more or less explicitly. In fact the references to Psalms 22 and 69 are so numerous that it has sometimes been suggested that the entire Passion narrative should be regarded as a kind of commentary on these two descriptions of the fate of the righteous sufferer.

We find it difficult to reply in a wholly satisfactory way to these critics without adopting one form or another of the hypothesis of the origin of the Passion narrative which we set out above. This makes it possible to do justice to the arguments of the sceptics: a liturgy is not concerned with legal accuracy or a probable chronology. It seeks to express the relentless hostility of all the authorities towards Jesus, without worrying about the forms that their attacks may have taken. It draws constantly upon scripture, and throughout seeks to show that the text of the ancient sacred books is applicable to the present-day situation. It spontaneously imposes its own chronological structure on events which it is more concerned to commemorate than to reconstruct. But at the same time, the liturgy of the Christian Passover at Jerusalem, which goes back to a very short time after the crucifixion, brings certain valuable guarantees. It cannot depart too much from topographical probability, even though the indications that it gives are sometimes less clear than later centuries alleged. It corresponds to the recollections of the principal witnesses of the events, or else it would have provoked embarrassing contradictions. It roughly respects the chronological order of events, even if it forces them into too narrow a framework. In short, though not a historical document of which it is easy to make us, it at least gives us some idea of the course of events in the last days of Jesus' life.

It is likely that the episode of the anointing at Bethany, which is lacking in Luke, nevertheless formed an integral part of the earliest Passion narrative, for it is found in John just before the beginning of the Passion (12.1–8), and it seems as though the author of the Fourth Gospel was inspired by it to produce the episode of the washing of the feet, which replaces the narrative of the Last Supper in his gospel (13.1ff.). The omission of this anecdote in Luke is probably due to his preference for the similar narrative of the forgiveness of the sinful woman which he gives in 7.36–50. Similarly, the agreement of the three synoptic narratives, and the mention of a meal in John 13.2, tip the balance in favour of an account of the Last Supper in the primitive narrative, for the celebration of a community meal on the pattern of that of Jesus and his disciples can be expected at the beginning of a liturgy commemorating the martyrdom of the Lord. The connection established in I Cor. 11.23ff. between the Christian supper and the last meal of Jesus confirms this hypothesis, for here Paul is quoting an ancient tradition which likewise links them with each other. What some critics regard as a difficulty, the presence of a liturgical fragment in a historical narrative, ceases to be so if the whole passage is liturgical in origin. In the rest of the narrative, there is no reason to exclude any of the important episodes, although a number of narrative ornamentations do not belong to the primitive document. The same is true of Luke 22.24–38 and the farewell discourses in John (13.12 to 17.26). They are substantially due to the redactional work of the evangelists, especially in the case of John, Luke being content here to group together ancient traditions which he drew from elsewhere. Finally, in spite of a current opinion which connects the narrative of the empty tomb with the visions of the risen Christ, we believe that the recounting of the women's adventure forms the triumphal conclusion of the liturgy of the Passion. The Easter event was not narrated during the first generation, as is proved by the late character of all the stories of appearances of the risen Christ and, even more, of the accounts of the resurrection; it was *affirmed*, as the angel affirms it here (Mark 16.6), and some of its consquences were included as *signs* of what had happened, as in the case of the empty tomb. The Christian pilgrims had no need of anything more in order to be strengthened in their faith.

Such were the dimensions of this first Passion narrative. It does not seem to have been formed with the aim that it should be systematically committed to memory. It may have been written down quite soon. In any case, its wording was not rigidly fixed, if one is to judge by the considerable differences which exist, behind the same general structure, between the narrative of Mark and that of Luke, which are relatively faithful reproductions of two different branches of the tradition. All that remained stable were the order of events and the main outlines of each episode. The liturgical indications, such as the mention of the time, and the innumerable allusions to passages in the Psalms, had a tendency to disappear gradually to make way for less rigid indications of time and explicit quotations of scripture, more compatible with a purely narrative style and with the progress of Christian exegesis. A comparison between the four narratives of the crucifixion (Mark 15.22–39 par.) makes this very clear. But it would be idle to suppose that the original document can be reconstructed word for word as it existed behind the evolution of the tradition, for with the passage from Aramaic to Greek and from liturgy to narrative, the lack of rigidity which was characteristic of this narrative from the first could only increase.

Thus we believe that it is an illusion to attempt to reconstruct on the basis of the gospel Passion narratives a precise historical account of the course of Jesus' martyrdom. The date of the Last Supper, of the arrest of Jesus and of the crucifixion are facts which we shall never be able to establish with certainty. The studies of Annie Jaubert (cf. above p. 5) and the discussions which followed their publication have simply made it clear that the chronology of the gospel narratives is even more questionable than had been thought, and that the Last Supper and the arrest of Jesus may have preceded the crucifixion by a longer period than the gospels suggest. As for the choice between 14 and 15 Nisan as the day of Jesus' execution, that is, between the chronology of John and that of the synoptics, it is made no easier by the reconstruction of the archaic Jewish calendar which certain pious Jews preferred to that of the Jerusalem temple. At best one can say that Mlle Jaubert has done us the service of showing that this is not the essential question. It is idle to suppose that the question of the twofold trial of Jesus will one day be satisfactorily solved. The debate goes on for ever, and the inadequate documentation we possess makes any solution precarious.

On the other hand, the fact that the archetype of the Passion narratives is rooted in the life of the earliest church of Jerusalem is a guarantee that the essential facts are established with certainty: Jesus was arrested at Jerusalem, where he had come on the occasion of a Passover pilgrimage; he was the victim of an agreement between the rulers of the Temple and the Roman authorities; he was condemned to death by Pontius Pilate, prefect of Judaea – and not 'procurator'; for the *hēgemōn* of the gospels renders the Latin *praefectus*, as is proved by an inscription discovered at Caesarea in 1961. He suffered the horrible torture of the cross, generally reserved for slaves and lower-class rebels. His disciples and companions offered no serious resistance to his arrest and execution and seem to have fled and scattered, which meant that they did not share the lot of their Master. Similarly, some of the sites indicated are likely to be the actual ones, and some episodes may contain reliable memories, for, as we have said above, some authorized witnesses of the facts were members of the church of Jerusalem.

But the participation of the latter in the life of the community which created the archetype of the Passion narratives is a guarantee above all that what we have here is the impression produced upon the disciples by the martyrdom of Jesus. It is an impression which followed the resurrection, but which integrates the great shock of the catastrophe of Golgotha with the portrait of the Master that the same men preserved in the form of the tradition dating from the time when they accompanied him. Thus it is of immense interest to the biographer of Jesus.

First of all, the disciples thought that their Master was ready to sacrifice his life. The presence at the beginning of the Passion narrative of the episodes of the anointing at Bethany, the Last Supper, and the prayer of Gethsemane make this perfectly clear. The attitude of Jesus at the time of his arrest and his trial confirm it. Since certain dominical sayings tell us of the high position he accorded to suffering in human life, particularly for his disciples, this view is extremely probable. The disciples were also persuaded that Jesus gave a redemptive significance to his death: the words which they attributed to him at the Last Supper are perfectly clear in this respect, especially the saying concerning the blood. We shall not attempt here to go behind the variations which exist between the synoptics and I Cor. 11.23ff. in order to establish the primitive form of these words in the archetype of the Passion narrative and in historical reality. Joachim Jeremias has done this in his *Eucharistic Words of Jesus* in such careful detail that there is no need to return to the subject, except to say that he has definitely shown that there was a Semitic original behind the Greek of the New Testament texts. This makes untenable the thesis that the narrative of the Last Supper was a Hellenistic cult legend. It may nevertheless be that cultic use influenced these words from the first; thus we are obliged to admit that it is impossible to demonstrate their total authenticity or inauthenticity.

The disciples of Jesus placed on his lips on the occasion of this scene two sayings which prophesied his death, and made the actions of the head of the table into prophetic acts prefiguring and making inevitable the martyrdom that he was to undergo. They added a phrase claiming that the blood to be spilt would establish between God and his people the new covenant prophesied by Jeremiah 31.31ff. Although there is not the same guarantee of exact memorization in the case of these sayings as for those which occur in the body of the gospels, there is a good possibility that they are a fairly faithful echo of what the historical Jesus declared. It will be noted that they contain no exact definition of the relationship between the death of the Master and the covenant which they inaugurate. The fact that apart from Mark 10.45b and Matt. 20.28 they have virtually no parallel in the synoptic gospels no doubt indicates that this was not an element in the Master's preaching which the disciples recognized as essential. Such declarations, however fragile the chronology of the gospels may be supposed to be, were probably made towards the end of Jesus' ministry, when his life was more and more seriously menaced. But they must not be woven into an elaborate portrayal of the interior evolution of Jesus, for which there is little or no support in the texts.

The second important feature which the disciples recall in the drama of their Master's martyrdom is the element of the unexpected, of surprise, which it contained. There is a trace of defensiveness in the way in which the tradition has been strained in order to emphasize how serious was the resistance which the companions of Jesus offered at Gethsemane, and in order to attribute the ending of the struggle to an order by their Master (Matt. 26.51–56; Luke 22.49–51; John 18.10f.). The corresponding passage of Mark, surely closer to the original narrative, makes clear the derisory character of this resistance: a blow with the sword, a few resigned words from Jesus, who had already been made prisoner, and a general flight (Mark 14.47–50). A confirmation that the little group of Galileans was taken by surprise is to be found in the insistence of the narrative on the presence of a traitor at the place of arrest. Later, a scornful remark to Judas was attributed to Jesus (Matt. 26.50; Luke 22.48), or else there was an attempt to show that the intervention of Judas was to no purpose, since the arrest of the Master was possible only when he delivered himself to the terrified patrol (John 18.2–12). But the theme of betrayal, on which there is strong emphasis (Mark 14.10f., 18–21, 40–42 par.), certainly reflects the impression of surprise and consternation received by the disciples and perhaps by Jesus himself.

Another important theme which shows us one aspect of the impression produced upon these men by the tragic fate of their Master is that of the loneliness of Jesus in the face of death. The disciples were rapidly dismissed to the sidelines, in spite of their desire to share the lot of their leader (Mark 14.27–31, 37–41, 50–52, 54, 66–72; 15.4ff. par.). The part that they played is not shown in a particularly good light, and Peter's repentance after his denial shows that they reproached themselves bitterly. But their responsibility is not seriously under discussion, for their inability to follow their Master was the result of the will of God (cf. Mark 14.27–31 par.). The disciples would later be called to sacrifice their lives (cf. Mark 8.34f.), but it was not right that they should die with Jesus. Those who were crucified with Jesus were people of quite a different kind, who poured insults upon

73

him (Mark 15.32 par.; the conversion of the repentant thief in Luke 23.39–43 was added to the tradition later). The idea that the death of Jesus had a very special significance appears here; it recurs in a more developed form in the miraculous episodes which accompanied his agony and death (Mark 15.33 par.; Mark 15.38 par.; Matt. 27.51b–53) and in the effect produced by his death on the centurion (Mark 15.39 par.) and on the crowd (Luke 23.48). In the eyes of the disciples it was a cosmic event, the end of the ancient pattern of religion and a complete moral victory over the most stubborn enemy. Here we see the emergence of ideas which later Christian preaching and theology were to develop at length. In this first naïve form, they surely represent the reaction of the first disciples to the tragedy of the cross. They would not have been possible if these men had not had some Messianic convictions concerning their Master even before his arrest.

It is not necessary to stress at length the way in which, at Gethsemane, Jesus is presented as an example of submission to the will of God and of obedient prayer. This is an expression of the devotion of the primitive church. But it also proclaims the conviction that the perfect obedience of the Son to the Father was, as is that of the Christian to God, a conquest not to be achieved without effort. The image of Jesus here is the same as in the narrative of the temptation.

All the accusations made against Jesus during his trial are presented by the Passion narratives as crude lies (cf. for example Mark 14.55–64 par.), but this is rather a stylistic device than a plea or the expression of indignation. Nothing astonished the disciples in those who wanted to kill their Master. Moreover, everything is very vague here, including the accusation of blasphemy (Mark 14.63f. and Matt. 25.65f.). As for the political charges made when he appeared before Pilate, according to Luke 23.2 and John 18.29; 19.12, they give every impression of being explanatory comments on the wording of the notice placed above the cross of Jesus to show his crime, which, according to the unanimous testimony of all four gospels, bore the famous words 'King of the Jews'. In substance, this statement is highly likely to be in conformity with historical reality, for it would not have been created by a Hellenistic church with little wish to be involved in political problems, and it could not have been created by a Jerusalem church living in the middle of people who had seen the inscription. Thus it signifies that Jesus was condemned to death for political reasons. We shall return below (pp. 113ff.) to this fact, which the first Christians never sought to hide.

The silence maintained by Jesus during the greater part of his trial and execution is a feature which certainly goes back to the archetype of the Passion narrative. There is no explanation or comment upon it, and it may reflect the conviction that the Master had no need to lower himself to refute unfounded accusations and to protest against the maltreatment inflicted upon him. It may also be an echo of the portrait of the suffering servant in Isa. 53.7, but, as is well known, this verse is not quoted in the Passion narratives and there is no other clear allusion to it. This is a surprising fact, and should put us on our guard against the idea that the suffering of Christ may have a substitutionary and expiatory significance in these narratives. In them, the death of Christ is the founding of a new covenant, which is not quite the same thing.

Nevertheless, the Passion narratives attributed a few brief words to Jesus during his trial and execution. There is no need to emphasize that the community of believers had no official witness in the various places where these words were pronounced, and even if they had received information from the people who were there, such communications are far less certain than the content of sayings which have been systematically taught and memorized. The synoptic gospels give only one declaration of Jesus before the Sanhedrin (Mark 14.62 par.), while John 18.19–23 places on the Master's lips scathing replies, one to the high priest and the other to the servant who struck him. These two replies may have a historical content, but it is difficult to demonstrate this. In any case, they amount to a refusal on the part of Jesus to accept the authority of the illegal tribunal before which he had been brought. The reply which the synoptics attribute to the Master when the high priest asks if he is the Messiah is the same in structure in the three texts, but varies slightly from one to the other: after the first reply referring directly to the question, a second brings new information concerning the Son of man. According to Luke, the dialogue continued (Luke 22.70) amongst all the members of the Sanhedrin – to whom he already attributed the first question – and Jesus; but this more complex account seems to be secondary.

In Mark, Jesus' answer to the question 'Are you the Messiah?' is affirmative, in Matthew it is ambiguous, and in Luke it is nothing but a refusal to reply. The second part of the reply limits the first more or less clearly. There has been much scholarly discussion on this combination. Some critics[9] consider that here Jesus refused the title of Messiah in order to affirm that he was the Son of man, that is, a spiritual and not a political Messiah. This theory is difficult to defend, because it would be true only if the Master had replied 'No' in clear terms to the question put to him. Since the reply which we have is positive or ambiguous, the most reasonable thing is to assume that Jesus passed over his messianic dignity to come to the important matter, which is what he had to say about the Son of man. In Luke, we read that the Son of man is from now on to be seated at the right hand of God, while in Matthew and Mark the affirmation is a twofold one: that he is to sit at the right hand of God, like the Messiah of Psalm 110.1, and to come with the clouds as in Daniel 7.13. We have discussed above (pp. 45ff.) how Jesus' teaching on this Son of man must be understood. We believe that here the rather forced interpretation given to it by the early Christians has been integrated with the various forms taken by the Master's reply. All that can be affirmed is that Jesus may have drawn the attention of the members of the Sanhedrin to this aspect of his preaching, in order to prevent them from transforming the personal decision required of every one of them, with regard to his paradoxical Messianic status, into an intellectual game. The more or less overt threat contained in the Master's words may have been the essential element in his reply. Here again, having rather vague information, and not being very clear themselves on the meaning of the idea of the Son of man as Jesus spoke of it, the disciples have given us a reconstruction of what, from the knowledge they had of his preaching, the Master must have said. Once again, they present us with the portrait they had of a Jesus whose authority was assured, and who did not hesitate to stand up to the high priest in the full Sanhedrin, when at last he condescended to do so.

The synoptic gospels and John agree that Jesus did not

remain silent before Pilate. But the Fourth Gospel shows him exchanging almost philosophical remarks with Pilate (John 18.33–38; 19.8–11). Their redactional origin is obvious. The synoptics attribute to him only the ambiguous reply 'You have said so' to the prefect's question 'Are you the King of the Jews?' This brief dialogue probably belonged to the archetype of the Passion narrative, but is no more than a very reserved use of the title placed on the cross to show that while the responsibility for this inscription was Pilate's, Jesus had no objection to its content. The same attitude as in his reply to the high priest and in various other situations in his life is thus attributed to him: the Master condescended to accept the titles assigned to him, but showed considerable reserve when the person speaking to him did not draw for himself the conclusions which his declaration required (Mark 10.17f. par.; Matt. 7.21–23; etc.).

In Luke and in John, Jesus utters in each case three sayings during the crucifixion, at least if one accepts the longer text of Luke 23.34, which raises certain difficulties. In both gospels he is presented as the model of the dying man who forgives and does good to those around him (Luke 23.34; 23.42; John 19.26f.), and then at the last moment submits humbly and with confidence to the will of God (Luke 23.46; John 19.28, 30). This is an edifying portrait which may go back to the two forms of the Passion narrative used by these evangelists, but certainly not to the archetype, since Matthew and Mark attribute to Jesus, apart from the great cry with which he dies, only a single saying (Mark 15.34 and Matt. 27.46): a brief quotation from Psalm 22, of which they give the Hebrew text in an approximate transcription into Greek letters. The liturgical origin of this detail can hardly be questioned. No doubt the community gathered at Jerusalem recited Psalm 22 at this point, evoking the sufferings of the persecuted righteous man, and then his final triumph. This does not rule out the historical authenticity of the story; but it would be as hard to prove as the reverse. In our view, what matters is that the disciples, on the basis of what they had learned of their Master, had the conviction that in his utmost distress he had remained certain that God would vindicate him even beyond death. In saying this with so impressive a degree of reticence, they were certainly affirming the resurrection of their Lord, but doing so not by sounding the trumpets

77

of paschal rejoicing, but simply by taking up ideas set forth by the Master when he was alive, especially when he was talking of the suffering of the Son of man. In this way they show us how they apprehended this aspect of Jesus' message.

As we have said, the part played by the Jewish and Roman authorities is presented in a confused fashion in the Passion narratives. What is clear, however, is the low opinion the narrators have of the courage, honesty and nobility of the great ones of this world. Even when apologetic motives have favoured Pilate, as is the case in the Fourth Gospel at least, the portrait we receive of these hate-filled or blind nonentities is no more than a blacker version of that which Jesus drew of them in his preaching (Mark 10.42 par.; Luke 13.31–33; Matt. 6.1ff.). This indicates that the Master's radical freedom of speech had been understood by the disciples, who no longer cared to lavish on the authorities the marks of respect that the generation which followed would once again consider indispensable.

The episode of Barabbas (Mark 15.6–15 par.) and the presence of the two 'robbers' at Golgotha on one side and the other of Jesus, forces us amongst other things to ask how the disciples regarded the relationship between their Master and the more violent of his contemporaries. We shall return to this question below pp. 118ff., and shall do no more here than to make one or two observations on the Passion narrative. By presenting Jesus as executed by the Romans on political grounds, the first narrators knew that they would provoke a reaction of sympathy amongst many Palestinian Jews of their period, a reaction based on the general hatred for the occupiers. By speaking also of Barabbas 'among the rebels in prison, who had committed murder in the insurrection' (Mark 15.7), 'a notorious prisoner' (Matt. 27.16), 'who had been thrown into prison for an insurrection started in the city, and for murder' (Luke 23.19) or, more simply, a 'robber' (John 18.40), and of the two brigands on Golgotha, who were perhaps also popular Robin Hoods, the gospel narratives were indicating that there were two ways of defending the rights of the Jewish people: that which led to murder and to the execution of an innocent man and which was implicitly blamed in spite of the popularity; and that of Jesus, misunderstood at first, but bringing in the end a much more complete revolution.

The most striking symbol of this revolution is the centurion at Golgotha. This Roman officer, the responsible representative of the occupying power in its most inflexible form, surpasses Pilate in his supernatural clairvoyance. Whereas the prefect had affirmed, in purely political terms, that Jesus was Messiah, by describing him as 'King of the Jews', the centurion proclaimed, according to Luke, the innocence of the crucified Jesus (Luke 23.47) and, according to Mark and Matthew, that he was Son of God (Mark 15.39 and Matt. 27.54), whatever meaning may be given to this term. In other words, the centurion rejects the condemnation passed on this king of the Jews, accepting the legitimacy of his claims in the face of all the powers who had sent him to his death. This officer is not converted; he does not become a deserter; he is there to utter the only honest judgment on the poor condemned man, and this prepares the way for the great divine rehabilitation of the resurrection, and for the triumphant preaching which will follow it. The fact that it is not the disciples who fulfil this role is important for the knowledge of the historical Jesus: the companions of the Master show in this way that they do not claim a monopoly of the knowledge of Jesus (cf. Mark 9.38–40 par.). We shall see that there are even clearer traces in the gospels of this attitude, which they learnt from Jesus.

The two final episodes of the earliest Passion narrative are those which conclude the Gospel of Mark: the deposition in the tomb (Mark 15.42–47 par.) and the discovery by the women of the empty tomb (Mark 16.1–8 par.). These accounts are so obviously complementary that it is astonishing to see some critics separating them. Together they form so fine a conclusion to the liturgy of the commemoration of the Passion that they should not be studied independently of the rest of this text. Here as elsewhere, the question of the historicity of the events which they relate is insoluble. What is clear, however, is the impression which according to Mark this twofold scene made upon those who witnessed it. Unquestionably dead, Jesus was buried in a cave-tomb; two days later, not only had his body disappeared, but a divine messenger was telling the women who wanted to do again what had already been done at Bethany that the risen Master was already on his way. After the silent despair of the deposition in the tomb, we have here a mute terror in the face of the inexplicable. Whatever one may say, there is no trace here of any systematic reflection or apologetic argument in any of this, especially if the two or three Marcan additions, 15.44b–45 and 16.7, are removed from the passage. The resurrection simply demonstrates the action of God and consequently gives a meaning to the whole Passion: the Father has vindicated the Son, but human beings find that this divine intervention, which announces the end of their world, is beyond their understanding. The period of intimacy with the Master (Mark 15.40f.) is over. This is an indirect proof of the previous existence of a small group of companions of Jesus, which no longer had any reason to exist when it was separated from its leader.

In short, the Passion narrative deliberately concentrates attention on the person of the Lord. It gives us some indication, not only of the circumstances of his martyrdom, but also of the way in which his disciples understood that event: completely independent of the established authorities and of those who opposed and attached them, determined to maintain to the end the eschatological character of his message and his mission, Jesus is the persecuted righteous man whose final triumph is assured in spite of everything, including abandonment by his own friends. In dying, he becomes the paradoxical 'King of the Jews' whose victory is a threat to the very foundations of the existing order. In order to explain what happened on Good Friday, the post-resurrection faith borrows here for this purpose much material which goes back to the Jesus of history.

6

The Jesus of the Parables

The frontier between the parables and the dominical sayings is not as clear as one might think. In fact the word *parabolē* does not always carry in the gospels the meaning we usually give it, that of an account of a particular case intended to support an argument from analogy, which finds its ideal application in long narrative parables such as those of the Good Samaritan or the Talents. This use of the term, which corresponds to that of ancient Greek rhetoric, is particularly frequent in Matthew and Luke, where it is clearly redactional in origin, and occurs in particular in the introduction to narrative parables (cf. e.g. Matt. 13.25; 21.33; 22.1; Luke 12.16; 15.3; 18.1; 19.11; 20.9). But there are other uses of the word *parabolē*, which seem to be older. The word may refer to the description of a natural phenomenon, and this is already a departure from the rules laid down by Aristotle in his *Rhetoric*, according to which it should refer to human examples (Mark 4.30 and Matt. 13.31). It may refer to a very general case described in a few words, without the least recourse to narrative (e.g. Luke 4.23; 6.39). It may also refer to a maxim with no appeal to the argument from analogy (e.g. Mark 7.15 par.).

This variety of uses would be confusing if there was not a very simple explanation for it. In the Septuagint, *parabolē* is the regular translation of the term *māshāl*, which has various meanings, including all those which we saw differed from Greek usage. It is clear that in the synoptic tradition the Greek word has been used to translate *māshāl*, or rather its Aramaic equivalent *mᵉthal*, which was used to describe all the teaching of Jesus which was in gnomic form, that is, a good part of the sayings which we included under the heading of 'dominical sayings'. As the tradition was Hellenized, and especially when the evangelists acquired a veneer of literary style, as in the case of Matthew and especially Luke, the Greek usage of the word *parabolē* gradually spread without completely eliminating the original meanings of the term. This is the reason for the confusion which we notice and the problems which the interpretation of *parabolē* poses in certain passages, in particular in Mark. It seems in fact that on two occasions the word has been used in this gospel to refer to a quotation from scripture which has acquired almost the significance of a proverb (Mark 4.13 and 12.12), while it is never used to describe a narrative parable of any length. For the plurals used in connection with the stories of the sower and the wicked husbandmen probably refer to the succession of scenes of which both are composed (Mark 4.2, 10, 12, 13; 12.1 speak of *parabolai*).

In order not to repeat the content of the chapter on the dominical sayings, we shall restrict ourselves here to the images and narratives which are parables in the usual sense, and ignore those which fall more into the category of maxims, although the latter may naturally include the element of comparison or metaphor. Once again, it is worthwhile giving Bultmann's inventory.[1] With A. Jülicher, whose celebrated work on the parables put on a new basis the exegesis of this part of Jesus' teaching,[2] he makes a distinction between similitudes (*Gleichnisse*), parables in the strict sense, and narrative parables (*Parabeln*). The first of these categories includes utterances which are still on the boundary of the category of dominical sayings: sometimes the similitudes do not include a formula indicating the comparison.

Luke 17.7–10: Master and servant.
Luke 14.28–33: The tower and the war.
Luke 15.4–10 and Matt. 18.12–14: The lost sheep and the lost coin.
Luke 12.39f. and Matt. 24.43f.: The thief.
Luke 12.42–46 and Matt. 24.45–51: The faithful servant.
Luke 12.54–56: Signs of the times.
Luke 12.57–59 and Matt. 5.25f.: Timely agreement.

Other similitudes include a more or less developed comparison, which, however, is no doubt the creation of the evangelist in some cases:

Matt. 11.16–19 and Luke 7.31–35: Children at play.
Mark 4.30–32; Matt. 13.31f.; Luke 13.18f.: The mustard seed.
Matt. 13.33 and Luke 13.20f.: The leaven.
Mark 4.26–29: The seed growing of itself.
Matt. 13.44: The treasure hidden in a field.
Matt. 13.45f.: The pearl of great price.
Matt. 13.47–50: The fishing net.
Matt. 7.24–27 and Luke 6.47–49: The house built on rock and the house built on sand.
Mark 13.28f. par.: The fig tree.
Mark 13.34–37: The returning householder.

Parables properly so called contain a narrative, but the frontier between this category and the previous one, or between that and dominical sayings which suggest an analogy with the human situation, is sometimes difficult to trace. Thus Matt. 7.9f. or Mark 3.27 are on the way to being narratives, but do not approach the length of a narrative parable. It is also possible to distinguish amongst parables in the strict sense a certain number of narratives in which an aspect of human behaviour is given as an example of what ought or ought not to be done, or where the analogy amounts to: 'Do (or do not do) likewise':

Luke 10.30–37: The good Samaritan.
Luke 12.16–21: The rich fool.
Luke 16.19–31: The rich man and Lazarus.
Luke 18.10–14: The Pharisee and the publican.

According to Bultmann, Luke 14.7–11 and 14.12–14 can be included amongst these brief narratives, and this seems reasonable, as the summons to imitation is the same in both cases. Finally, there are the following narrative parables:

Luke 11.5–8: The importunate friend.
Luke 18.1–8: The unjust judge.
Mark 4.3–9 par.: The sower.
Luke 13.6–9: The barren fig tree.

Luke 14.16–24 and Matt. 22.2–14: The banquet.
Luke 15.11–32: The prodigal son.
Luke 16.1–8: The unjust steward.
Matt. 25.14–30 and Luke 19.12–27: The talents.
Matt. 25.1–13: The ten virgins.
Matt. 13.24–30: The wheat and the tares.
Matt. 18.23–36: The unmerciful servant.
Matt. 20.1–16: The labourers in the vineyard.
Mark 12.1–9 par.: The wicked husbandmen.
Luke 7.41–43: The two debtors.
Matt. 21.28–31: The two sons.

Jülicher seemed to have said the last word about the interpretation of the parables. During the first third of the twentieth
century, his thesis went unchallenged and dominated the
debate concerning these familiar and yet difficult texts. He
seemed to have established definitively, in the face of the ancient allegorical interpretation which looked for a hidden meaning in every detail, the idea that every picture or narrative had
only a single 'point' and gave support to a single idea, usually
deriving from a kind of extremely general bourgeois morality.
However, with the famous book by C. H. Dodd, *The Parables
of the Kingdom*,[3] a reaction took place. This showed that
while Jülicher's destruction of the traditional exegesis of the
parables remained unchallenged, his own interpretation lacked
finesse and flexibility. There were some who sought to re-
habilitate the allegorical interpretations of the earliest com-
mentators, and an attempt was made to prove that this had
Jewish antecedents (M. Hermaniuk, H. Riesenfeld, etc.).
Many other critics tried in all kinds of ways to restore to the
parables the spiritual profundity which Jülicher had taken
away from them (W. Michaelis, J. J. Vincent, E. Linnemann,
D. Via, etc.). The most remarkable contribution to this re-
opening of the debate was and remains the work of Joachim
Jeremias *Die Gleichnisse Jesu*.[4]
The great merit of Jeremias' book was to state in full the
problem of the transmission of the parables before they reached
a fixed form in the gospels, and to show how a change in their
audience led to a twisting of the meaning rather than to
modifications of form. A parable told to a Jewish audience by

84

Jesus could have been preserved without very much apparent change. But once it became the object of instruction in the church, it became the vehicle of Christian preaching and thereby acquired a new meaning, this being permitted by the flexibility of its allusive and symbolic language. For example the parable of the faithful servant (Luke 12.42–46 and Matt. 24.45–51), a severe warning given by Jesus to the leaders of the people of Israel at the approach of the kingdom of God, became in the church an appeal to believers to prepare for the parousia of their Lord by living their faith actively. Another case is the parable of the wicked husbandmen, which was also addressed to the Jewish leaders, to proclaim to them the loss of their privileges and the handing over of their function to others. In the Christian church it became an allegory of the history of salvation, in which the son of the householder represents Jesus Christ, while the servants sent before him are identified with the prophets. We should add that Jeremias makes good use of a number of parables found in the apocryphal Gospel of Thomas discovered at Nag Hammadi in Egypt after the Second World War, in order to reconstruct the primitive form of these sayings of Jesus. In the canonical gospels we sometimes have a more developed version than in the Gospel of Thomas. This is so for the parables of the wicked husbandmen or of the great banquet.

The brilliant critical work of Jeremias was a remarkable step forward in the study of the parables, and many of his conclusions can be accepted without question. It has, in our view, two limitations which make it necessary for study to be continued. The historical framework within which each parable was pronounced by Jesus seems sometimes to be stated both too exactly and too vaguely; while the problem of transmission is well stated but not satisfactorily resolved. With regard to the original historical setting, Jeremias confidently identifies those to whom the Master was speaking, on the basis of a number of indications in the parables themselves. But one sometimes hesitates to follow him, since the indications on which they are based seem extremely vague. At the same time, he hardly ever asks what circumstances would have favoured the utterance by Jesus of declarations of this kind. By no means every setting was appropriate to this. Secondly, Jeremias hardly discusses the technique of transmission, the spread of the parables within the churches and outside them, and the reasons why there are much more profound differences within the synoptic gospels with regard to the parables than in the case of the dominical sayings and the conflict dialogues. In our view these differences must form a starting point.

Half the parables which we find in the Gospel of Luke are peculiar to it. In general, the tone is that of moral exhortation. The narrative parables, like the other narratives in this gospel, have a markedly emotional side to them (cf. the Prodigal Son, in Luke 15.11–32). It seems certain that Luke found these parables in the *preaching* of the churches where he gathered his material, and that they served as illustrations and examples for a message which emphasized piety, religious emotion and a morality based upon repentance and forgiveness.

In the Gospel of Matthew, almost half the parables have no parallel in the other canonical gospels. Many of the parables peculiar to Matthew, as well as several of those which he shares with Luke, or with Mark and Luke, are highly allegorized and very eschatological. The place of the 'parables of the kingdom' in this group is well known. The texts in question give the impression of having been discussed, interpreted and sometimes reformulated in a theological school comparable in some respects to the rabbinic schools. In any case, they have received their final formulation in the framework of *theological study or teaching* (cf. Matt. 13 or Matt. 25).

Whatever the exact date of the final composition of the Gospel of Mark, it in any case takes us much closer to the starting point of Christian oral tradition. Thus one might suppose that it would give us information about a very early stage in the history of the parables. Unfortunately, it contains only a few parables, and neglects most of those we know in Matthew and Luke. Why is this so, when there is no reason to think that most of these texts are late creations? It will be noted that the question is even more puzzling with regard to the Fourth Gospel. 'Mark' may not have known the parables, or at least not all of them, but to assume that this ignorance was shared by two evangelists who otherwise differ so much, with regard to texts which were so easy to present to their readers, is hardly a satisfactory explanation. There must certainly be other reasons, the most likely of which is a lack of interest, rather than any categorical rejection.

It is indeed difficult to see what the evangelist Mark could have found to object to in most of the parables. Moreover, if he had had serious reserves about them, he would have been unlikely merely to leave them aside quietly. We have a good indication of his attitude in the case of the parable of the sower (Mark 4.3ff.). Of course, this is not the place to become deeply involved in the difficult dispute about the relationships between the text of the parable (4.3–9), the allegorical interpretation of the text which is found in vv. 13–20 and the remarks concerning 'the parables' found in vv. 10–12. Most critics accept that vv. 13–20 are the work of the evangelist, or of the church whose spokesman he was. They must be attributed to the evangelist himself at the time of the redaction of his book. But what of vv. 10–12? Some, including Jeremias, regard them as an independent *logion*, inserted here by the evangelist, who wrongly saw them as a general theory of parables. Others, including Bultmann, see them as the creation of the evangelist, who wished to state this theory. In any case, both views agree that these verses must have been placed there deliberately by the author of the Gospel of Mark. In our view, both theses are equally false. The evangelist Mark's theory of parables is set out at the end of the collection of which the parable of the sower is the first, in 4.33f., and it differs considerably from what we read in 4.10–12, since it regards this literary category as the essence of elementary teaching. Verses 10–12 are an ancient explanation of the series of 'parables' of the sower which Mark did not dare pass over in silence because it was too well known. Thus he followed it with his own personal explanation, but in v. 13 began by aiming a serious blow at 'those who were about Jesus with the twelve', whom he held responsible for the earlier interpretation, too esoteric for his liking.

The group to which 'Mark' gave that rather unusual name had supplied him with the story of the sower. It had been the agent for the transmission of this parable at least, and perhaps also of the other main parables in Mark, which likewise have something academic about them: a quotation from scripture (or an allusion to it); a comparison with the kingdom of God or with another passage of scripture (4.26–29; 4.30–32;

12.1–11). Once again we meet a Christian rabbinic milieu of the kind which handed down Matthew's parables, no doubt at an earlier phase in its development. A group in the church of Jerusalem must at some time have developed an interest in the parables of Jesus, beginning with the smaller number of them which suited its exclusive tendencies. The author of the Gospel of Mark tries to bring this enterprise to a halt by showing the real meaning of the parables interpreted in an esoteric sense by this group.

The problem remains, however, of the large number of parables neglected by Mark. Why was the evangelist not attracted by these portraits and narratives, which enchanted all later Christian generations? Could he not have appreciated at their true value the traditions which he regarded as a kind of teaching for the use of the multitude, since he had such missionary enthusiasm himself? This is to ignore the fact that Mark does not recount the teaching of Jesus in detail and is very reticent with regard to the content of the Master's popular preaching (1.15). For the purpose which he had set himself, what mattered was the activity of Jesus and what he set out to teach his disciples.

If the greater part of the parables had been understood by those amongst whom he lived as instruction meant for the 'disciples', i.e. members of the church, it is certain that Mark would have given us more of them. Consequently, at this period they were regarded as something other than the communications to the faithful which they later became. Can we then follow the evangelist Mark and admit that they were in fact teaching which Jesus meant for the multitude? There are some difficulties in this. Certainly Jesus' contacts with the multitude sometimes took the form of teaching. But preaching to large crowds cannot include many nuances and subtleties, and the parables are full of these. Of course, some of the narrative parables may have been illustrations of statements addressed to the multitude. This is particularly true of certain narratives in the parables peculiar to Luke, though they may have had other uses. But how can parables like those of Matthew 13, or the unfaithful steward, have formed part of teaching addressed to the multitude? And how could we explain why the parables came so slowly to form part of the tradition which the evangelists gathered together – as is shown by the differences between the gospels with regard to them – if they had been known as an integral part of Jesus' preaching to the multitude? Finally, in the eyes of the multitude, as we shall see, Jesus was a healer and a more or less Messianic personality. In the tumult which surrounded this famous man, of which we find many examples in the gospels (cf. Mark 5.25ff.), the opportunities for preaching to large crowds cannot have been very frequent, and occasions such as that portrayed in Mark 4.1f. must have occurred a great deal less often than the scenes recounted in Mark 3.9ff. and 6.54–56. If we turn from the life of the Master to that of the primitive church, it does not seem that it made any more use of parables in preaching to the multitude: neither the first chapter of Acts, nor the epistles of Paul, nor those of James and Peter, to the extent to which they echo the preaching of the first two leaders of the church at Jerusalem, give us the least indication of this. Thus the idea that the parables may have been essentially a form of popular teaching was an invention made for apologetic purposes by the evangelist Mark, aimed at combatting a first attempt to integrate this literary form into the church tradition.

This first attempt, which finds expression in Mark 4.10–12, and is applied to the parable of the sower, starts from two postulates. First of all, it assumes that the parable was created by Jesus, and there is no reason to dispute this, even if one thinks that one or other of the gospel parables may be more recent or may have been borrowed from Jewish folklore. Secondly, it considers parables as teaching concerned above all with 'those outside', whose hearts were hardened and were not saved by the preaching of Jesus. The impression one has is of a somewhat laborious retort, meant to convince the members of the church that they were better informed than anyone else, even though they had no monopoly of the preservation of the sayings of Jesus. Those outside may have had access to the Master's teaching, but this was of no value to their salvation – quite the contrary.

This leads us to ask the following question. If part of the teaching of Jesus was transmitted outside the church, if moreover the parables entered the gospel tradition only gradually, and if the discussion of the situation of 'those outside' turned on a few parables, must it not be admitted that the transmission of the parable took place at first outside the group of the disciples, and then outside the church of the first generation, before gradually finding its way into the church during the second and third generations? It is clear that the form of the parables does not show the marks of any attempt at systematic memorization, and that their transmission was not as firmly guaranteed as that of the dominical sayings. Thus one cannot attribute to the Master any initiative aimed at ensuring the unaltered transmission of these scenes and narratives, even if one acknowledges that he was the author of most of them. Those who heard Jesus must have noted or learnt by heart the main features of the parables, without having become on this account his disciples or having entered the Christian church. From what we have said, it is clear that they did not represent an organized group, but a sociological milieu within which some people took the initiative, being certain of arousing the interest of others by recounting these scenes and narratives.

What could this milieu have been? Jesus, a small village craftsman, seems to have recruited his disciples, or some of them at least, from the social classes close to his own: master fishermen from the sea of Tiberias (Mark 1.16–20 par.), tax collectors (Mark 2.14 par.). His closest relationships were with this class and the class immediately above them, even if he often moved in the humblest circles, particularly those of the peasants of Galilee. Amongst these lower-middle-class and middle-class people who supplied most of the members of the Pharisee party, but who also included a good number of black sheep – tax collectors or shady business men (cf. Luke 16.1ff.) – the Master was unquestionably popular. He was often invited for meals in the houses of members of these groups, as the gospels frequently note: meals with the disciples, of course (Mark 1.29–31 par.; Mark 2.15), or with close friends (Luke 10.38–42; John 12.1–8), but also with Pharisees who were not followers of his (Luke 7.36f.; 11.37ff.; 14.1ff.) and also with tax collectors or still unconverted 'sinners' (Mark 2.16 par.; Luke 19.1ff.). He was interested in the customs which governed formal meals (Luke 14.7–14; 14.16–24 par.). The invitations which Jesus received in this way and often accepted seem certain to have been due in many cases to simple curiosity about his person.

But these people were also attracted, we feel, by the Master's talent for narrative. This unusual prophet was also a brilliant conversationalist, who knew how to seize an opportunity to recount an anecdote or evoke situations familiar to his hearers. He travelled a good deal throughout the region, knew everyone there and had an unequalled power of drawing an unexpected lesson from what seemed no more than an everyday fact, or of portraying in a telling fashion behaviour which was so strange, against the familiar setting, that it made people think. In short, we believe that most of the parables were part of the conversation at meals in the houses where Jesus had been invited. They may sometimes seem very severe or even aggressive for statements made at table, but that is what they were. Rather mysterious epigrams (Mark 4.26–29; 4.30–32 par.; Matt. 13.44; 13.45f.; etc.) were uttered side by side with fluent or picturesque narratives in which an attentive hearer would be aware that a surprising point was being made, while many would see it only as an odd or tragic story (Luke 10.30–37; 15.11–32; 16.1–8; Matt. 20.1–16 par.; 22.2–14 par.; 25.14–30 par.; etc.).

This conclusion may seem surprising. We believe, however, that it is fully supported by the content of the parables. We might first note that the theme of a meal is a fairly common one in them, which may indicate that they were uttered at table (Luke 11.5; 12.19; 14.7–11; 14.12–14; 14.16–24 par.; 15.16, 23, 27, 29f; 16.19–31; 17.7–10). But even more significant is the picture they give of social life. The rural aspect of the narratives and scenes portrayed by the Master has often been noted, and rightly so. One can also point to the extent to which society is seen here from the point of view of people who were comparatively well off. Of course social criticism is not absent: the unjust judge (Luke 18.1–8) is not shown in a very edifying light. The rich are criticized (Matt. 25.24) or threatened with eternal punishment (Luke 16.19–31; cf. Luke 12.16–21). But this criticism does not go very far, and does not go beyond what those who sat down with Jesus could have approved: a judge must be just and a rich person must not live in great luxury. In a general way, we meet a world where people have property (apart from the rich people mentioned above, cf. Luke 15.11–32; 16.1–8; 19.12–27 par.; Matt. 20.1–16; etc.); where people can afford to build (Matt. 7.24–27 par.; Luke 14.28–30), employ labour by the day (Matt. 20.1–16) or permanent workmen (Luke 17.7–10; Matt. 24.45–51 par.; Luke 13.7; 14.16ff. par.; 16.1–8; Matt. 25.14–30), obtain a considerable amount of capital in case of need (Matt 13.44–46; Luke 15.11–13), lend out money at a good rate (Luke 16.1–18; Matt. 25.14–30 par.), etc. There is a mention here and there of large absentee landlords in the background (Luke 16.1ff.; Mark 12.1–9 par.), but there is no particular criticism of them. The role of the villain is almost always played by social inferiors (Matt. 24.48–51 par.; Luke 16.1–8; Matt. 25.18, 24ff. par.; 18.23–36; 20.11ff.; Mark 12.1–9 par.). When they do well, they have a right to their master's congratulations (Luke 12.43f. par.; 16.8; 17.7–10; Matt. 25.20–23 par.). Of course in a situation of social immobility such as that of the Roman Empire, such an attitude is a general one, and does not necessarily associate the storyteller with a particular property-owning class. It is nevertheless striking in a person whom his disciples described as endowed with a unique independence and authority. We must conclude that in this case Jesus adapted himself to his middle-class hearers and that in addition he was understood by them in an even more conservative sense, corresponding to their own aspirations.

Amongst this group, very influential amongst the Jewish people, the parables which he told were preserved for some time, as a good example of how to say something wise and interesting in a relatively light form. The disciples, to whom these anecdotes and similitudes seemed of little importance, finally came to be interested in them and gradually to integrate the parables into Christian teaching, sometimes at the price of serious alterations, in addition to those introduced, in accordance with their own point of view, by the people who first handed them on. That is to say, there is a risk of a distortion in the portrait of Jesus reflected in these texts. On the other hand, their handing on by people who did not belong to the group of the disciples is a very useful check for the historian.

We have said what is necessary about the social attitude attributed to Jesus by the parables. We must turn now to the other aspects of the portrait of the Master reflected in them. Once again, we shall not inquire into the authenticity of each parable, for no satisfactory criterion exists. Of course, one may assume that there was a certain tendency towards an increasing allegorization of the parables, but this is a process which had not gone very far before the redaction of the gospels, while certain of the parables may have been considerably marked by allegory from the first, since the rabbis sometimes used this literary form. It is sufficient to say that the change of audience was a general one, and that virtually all the parables of Jesus were spoken to middle-class Jews before becoming, in the church tradition, and especially in the gospels, an integral part of the teaching addressed to Christians within the church. As a result, one must expect a more or less perceptible shift in their meaning, even though it is not always possible to distinguish it with certainty.

The Jesus of the parables, a skilled narrator, who was often speaking to people who had to be entertained before any message could be got over to them, certainly uttered parables which were quite ordinary in content and very elementary in their morality. Jülicher has been severely criticized for pointing this out, and for having tried to place all the parables at this level. However justifiable these criticisms were, if only on account of the sonorous platitudes which the famous biblical scholar borrowed from his own milieu in order to attribute them to Jesus, they were often excessive. There are in fact some parables in which the primary meaning is that of commonsense morality, and into which it is difficult to introduce a very inspiring religious message, even though this has been done in the course of the centuries. The saying concerning the necessity of coming to terms with one's adversary before going before the judge (Luke 12.58f. par.) is probably a parable which has gone unrecognized as such, as Bultmann argues. But even if it suggests an analogy with the necessity of reconciliation before the judgment of God, it is based upon an utilitarian morality which assumes that its original audience has its feet firmly on the ground. The parable of the house built on the rock and the house built on sand (Matt. 7.24–27 and Luke 6.47–49) seems very similar. Those of the two debtors (Luke 7.41–43) and the two sons (Matt. 21.28–31) are also examples of a commonsense morality which to all appearances formed part of Jesus' teaching, since the wisdom sayings, transmitted by a different

93

channel, contain their equivalent (Mark 3.24–26 par.; Matt. 6.22f. par.; Luke 6.43f. par.; etc.).

Sometimes the humorous and ironical nature of the parable obscures the fact that the ethical message is very simple. Parables such as that of the rich fool (Luke 12.16–21), the rich man and Lazarus (Luke 16.19–31), the importunate friend (Luke 11.5–8), the unjust judge (Luke 18.1–8), the unjust steward (Luke 16.1–8) and the talents (Matt. 25.14–30) are picturesque and amusing portraits of human behaviour in which the literary talent of Jesus reaches a high level and wins the attention of hearers with little commitment. But their point is so obvious and so elementary that it is virtually useless to emphasize it: nothing can protect us from death; we must pray with perseverance; the money one possesses must be put to use rather than turned into a problem in itself; etc. This is not to say that these teachings are of no account. They are part of the wisdom of nations, and it is interesting that in certain educated circles in Palestine at that time Jesus was understood as a wise man capable of saying in a skilful way what everyone knows, but must always learn again. Other parables give an emotional rather than an ironical or picturesque touch to the rules of perennial wisdom: the good Samaritan (Luke 10.30–37) is of course more than this, but nevertheless belongs to this category. So do the barren fig tree (Luke 13.6–9) and the prodigal son (Luke 15.11–32), about which one can say the same as about the good Samaritan. Thus the Jesus of the parables is amongst other things a preacher of universal morality.

However, in many cases the parables also contain a more direct religious teaching, which, though it is not entirely original, has some very distinctive features. It is obvious that in the background of many of these scenes and narratives is the figure of God the creator, law-giver and judge. Even if one rejects all allegorization of the parables, the analogy with the action of God has to be recognized in the behaviour of the householders and fathers who appear in them, especially if one accepts that these figures do not represent Jesus himself, contrary to what the evangelists often imagine. This almighty God, who gives life and takes it away (Luke 12.20), who is the absolute lord over man (Luke 17.7–10) and demands from him a certain return – the word is not too strong (Matt. 25.14–30 par.), in con-

94

formity with rules of conduct fixed by him alone (Matt. 7.24–27 par.), is also the God of forgiveness (Luke 18.10–14), of compassion (Luke 18.7), consolation for those whose life has been wretched (Luke 16.19–31), of extravagant generosity (Matt. 18.23ff.; 20.1–16; Luke 15.20ff.), of extremely bountiful reward (Matt. 25.21, 23), of patience (Luke 13.6–9; Matt. 13.24–30). It is this benevolent aspect of his being which is characteristic of him as he is portrayed by the Jesus of the parables. It seems clear that Jesus' hearers gained the impression that this was one of the original features in the message of this unusual guest.

But there is yet another dimension to the parables, through which we can perceive a portrait of the Master which does not limit his contribution to wisdom and to the message of the forgiveness of God. This is the eschatological dimension. Many of the parables, especially in the Gospel of Matthew, are 'parables of the kingdom', beginning with a formula such as: 'The kingdom of heaven is like . . .' However, many of these introductions may be the work of the redactor. More important is the fact that many of the parables radiate an extraordinary atmosphere, which is all the more striking in that it penetrates the most commonplace events of life and transfigures them without suppressing them. Thus we have the lost sheep or the lost coin (Luke 15.4–10 par.), which is sought to the exclusion of all else, a single-mindedness which is also found in the search for the hidden treasure or the pearl of great price (Matt. 13.44–46). The eschatological theme is also found in the return of the Master (Luke 12.42–46 par.; Mark 13.24 ff.; Matt. 25.14–30); in the coming of the bridegroom (Matt. 25.1–13), or of the thief (Luke 12.39f. par.); in the harvest (Mark 4.8f.; 4.26–29; Matt. 13.24–30) or in the gathering of the fruit (Mark 13.28f. par.; Luke 13.6–9; Mark 12.2 par.; Matt. 20.1–16; 21.28–31); in the rendering of accounts (Luke 16.1f.; Matt. 18.23; Luke 7.41–43); and in the banquet (Luke 14.16–24 par.) etc. All these were common images of the end of time and the coming of divine judgment. It seems clear that this atmosphere was deliberately created by the narrator and was understood by his hearers as an essential element in the parables.

Thus the message contained in these scenes and short narratives is not simply one of everyday morality, with a few distinctive features such as an insistence on the mercy of God. It is the proclamation that the narrator and his hearers are living in an exceptional situation, in which the end is already mysteriously present, even if it is also described as a future reality. If the behaviour of the persons in the parables sometimes takes an unexpected or even a bizarre turn, the reason is that God has begun to enter the world. His action amongst men can be perceived wherever abnormal behaviour is inspired by a single-minded passion: in the merchant who sells all for one pearl, in the gardener who lavishes toil upon the fruitless fig tree, in the father who loses his head at the return of the prodigal, in the king who remits enormous debts to his debtors. This passionate longing of God for men of course derives from a constant love for them, but at the moment when Jesus was speaking it had become particularly acute. Those who heard the parables do not seem to have read into what the Master said the least affirmation that his own person was in any way Messianic. Statements to this effect which are now found in them (Matt. 13.36ff.; Mark 12.6 par.) are obviously redactional. It is certain, however, that he who proclaimed God's passionate love for man and the imminent coming of the kingdom of God, was understood by those who heard him as himself belonging to the event of salvation which was more or less completely identifiable with his own activity.

Those who heard the parables provided Jesus with a very conventional framework of expression, and the Jesus whom they saw in what he taught was a somewhat pale figure. Yet he is the same person as the Master of the dominical sayings, though seen through different eyes.

7

The Jesus of the Miracle Stories

The miracle stories of the four canonical gospels have been the subject of innumerable controversies between those who have seen in them the proof of the divinity of Jesus, those who have sought for them a more or less natural explanation, those who have seen them as proving the non-historicity of the gospel, and many others beside. These absurd battles of words are still in progress, and even mar such scholarly studies as that of H. van der Loos.[1] We hope that we will be excused for not taking part in them, and asking instead the following questions: What role do these narratives play in the gospels, and how have they been adapted in order to fulfil it better? How were these narratives formed and handed on before the redaction of the gospels? What do they teach us about the impression produced by the Jesus of history?

A single glance at the canonical gospels is sufficient to confirm that the miracles of Jesus occupy an important place in them, and are the object of particular attention. The Gospel of Mark, the shortest of all, contains about twenty narratives attributing to Jesus actions regarded as contrary to the normal laws governing creation. In quantity, these narratives form more than a fifth of the work, that is, a little more than the Passion narrative. Miracles are mentioned in four of the general summaries which the evangelist uses to show that the anecdotes he recounts are only examples, and this shows that Mark wanted to emphasize the importance of these actions, although he resists the idea that they should be regarded as essential (Mark 1.32–34; 1.39; 3.7–12; 6.53–56). Similarly, the controversy of Mark 3.22–30 over the source of the exorcisms which Jesus carried out proves that the evangelist was seeking to show that although the Master was a miracle worker, he was not a magician. The miraculous anecdotes recounted by this gospel contain first of all three apophthegms in which the action of Jesus is less important than his words (2.1–12; 3.1–6; 7.24–30). In addition there are five acts which violate natural laws (4.35–41; 6.35–44; 6.45–52; 8.1–10; 11.12–14; 11.20–22); three exorcisms (1.23–28; 5.1–20; 9.14–29); six healings (1.29–31; 1.40–45; 5.25–34; 7.31–37; 8.22–26; 10.46–52); finally, a raising from the dead (5.21–24, 35–43).

The classification proposed here does not correspond to the data supplied by the texts and must not be taken too seriously. Nor does the way in which the stories are distributed throughout the gospel narrative provide any opportunity for a satisfactory classification, although this has sometimes been suggested.[2] All one can say is that in the eyes of the evangelist there is a close link between preaching and miracles – particularly exorcisms and healings – both in the ministry of Jesus during his lifetime and in the ministry which Christ carries out after the resurrection through the agency of his disciples (Mark 6.7–13). For him, a miracle is a guarantee that the preacher will not ignore the multitude, to whose needs it responds in a very precise way (Mark 1.32–34; 3.7–12; 6.35–44; 6.53–56; 8.1–10; 9.14ff.). It does not seem that he places a symbolic value on any kind of prodigy, except in the case of the double feeding of the multitude (6.35–44 and 8.1–10). A redactional commentary (8.15–21) makes this a symbol of the enrichment by generous sharing of the spiritual capital of the community. A more doubtful example is that of the healing of the blind man at Bethsaida (8.22–26), which, it has been suggested, may be a sign of the victory of Jesus over the spiritual blindness of the disciples. For Mark, the miracles of Jesus are purely and simply miracles which faith will allow the disciples to repeat in the same way (11.22–24).

In the Gospel of Matthew, the miracles of Jesus are more or less the same as in Mark: Matt. 9.27–34 and 12.22–24 are mere redactional additions intended to emphasize the sayings of the Master, while Matt. 8.5–13 and 17.24–27 really belong to the category of apophthegms, for the miracle is no more than an action intended to illustrate the teaching that is given there. A great effort is made by the evangelist to give a clear theological meaning to the miraculous acts of Jesus. The crudest narratives are suppressed (Mark 8.22–26), transformed into generalizing summaries which no longer contain anything shocking (Matt. 15.29–31 replaces Mark 7.31–37), or radically shortened (Matt. 8.28–34 corresponds to Mark 5.1–20). The miracles are repeatedly presented as the fulfilment of the Old Testament prophecies (Matt. 8.17; 11.4–6; 12.17–21). As H. J. Held has so clearly shown,[3] the Marcan narratives have been recast with a good deal of freedom in order to permit a symbolic interpretation of the miracles which particularly emphasizes the importance of faith (cf. Matt. 14.28–31). The doubling of the number of sick persons healed is a curious phenomenon which may be intended as a guarantee of the veracity of the miraculous act (8.28ff.; 9.27–31; 20.29ff.). It may also be a form of exaggeration of the miraculous, like the increasing of the number of people cured or helped (Matt. 8.16; 14.21; 15.38). In any case there is a very strong emphasis on the extraordinary aspect of Jesus' acts, which are those of a divine being.

In the Gospel of Luke, a number of Marcan stories have disappeared, perhaps because of their naïvety or their doubtful aspects (walking on the water, healings at Gennesaret, the Syro–Phoenician woman, the deaf mute, the second feeding of the multitude, the blind man at Bethsaida, the withered fig tree). On the other hand, a number of healing stories appear for the first time: the centurion's servant (7.1–10); the son of the widow of Nain (7.11–17); the woman who was bent over (13.10–17) and the man with dropsy (14.1–6), the latter two being concerned with the sabbath rest; the ten lepers (17.11–19). Note that with the exception of the episode of the widow's son, these stories all are the vehicles of some teaching on the part of Jesus, where the narrative is of secondary importance; that is, they are apophthegms of various kinds. Luke's miracle stories are longer than those of Matthew. The note of sentiment plays quite an important role, as in the rest of the gospel, with its general stylistic intention of edifying and appealing to the emotions. The miracles of Jesus are, of course, understood as the fulfilment of certain prophecies (cf. Luke 7.22), but this fact is not as important for Luke as it was for

99

Matthew. The dominating feature of the miracles is their nature as extraordinary events (Luke 5.26), their nature as prodigies demonstrating that Jesus is Messiah (Acts 2.22). In a general way, one may expect that all the miracle stories in Luke have been to some extent touched up to emphasize picturesque and emotional features.

Finally, in the Gospel of John, the miracle stories are fewer than in the synoptics, but perhaps play a more important part. There are seven: the marriage at Cana (2.1–11), the royal official (4.46–54), Bethsaida (5.2ff.), the feeding of the multitude (6.1–15), the walking on the water (6.6–21), the man born blind (9.1ff.), and the raising of Lazarus (11.1–44). In addition to these stories there are allusions to numerous other miracles performed by Jesus (2.23; 4.45; 11.47; 20.30), by which the evangelists may mean the other miracles recounted in the synoptic gospels. In fact, of the seven narratives in the Fourth Gospel, only three concern miracles known from the synoptics, and the way in which they are told is a good deal different (4.46–54; 6.1–15; 6.16–21). The stories this writer retains occupy an essential place in the first twelve chapters of the gospel. These chapters have been called the 'Book of Signs', from the name by which the miracles are known in this gospel. A few of them form the starting point of some of the most important discourses in the book, in chs. 5, 6 and 9. Moreover, the decisive turning points in the Master's career are marked on each occasion by a miracle (the marriage at Cana; the feeding of the multitude; the raising of Lazarus). In these circumstances, it is not surprising that they are all narrated in the evangelist's own style, for he was trying to endow them with the dignity of 'signs' comparable to those of the Old Testament. C. H. Dodd has shown, however, that John used traditions very similar to those to which the synoptic writers gave their final form, although they derived in part from other sources.[4] The hypothesis that the Johannine narratives were invented by the evangelist with the purpose of giving backing to his theological ideas is quite improbable.

From this very rapid study of the attitude of the four evangelists towards the miracle stories, we may conclude that it is in Mark that we may expect to find the versions closest to the original narratives, if one ignores the generalizing summaries which are the results of his redactional activity. What were these original narratives?

Mark sometimes modified the materials he used in order to introduce his own ideas. This has been the case in particular, it is claimed, for the theory of the 'Messianic secret', which was intended to explain the absence from the tradition of any claim that Jesus was Messiah. But the modifications introduced in this way into the miracle stories themselves seem to be very slight. The theme of the secrecy enjoined upon those who had been healed is not a frequent one (1.44; 5.43; 7.36; 8.26). Sometimes it is followed by the statement that the attempt to achieve secrecy failed (1.45; 7.36), and these statements give very much the impression of a redactor's conclusion correcting a traditional part of the narrative. On the occasion of some exorcisms Jesus also forbade the demons to speak (1.25, 34; 3.12), but this is mentioned only once within a narrative, and in the other two cases occurs in generalizing summaries. In 1.25 it certainly belongs to the original narrative, because it forms part of the techniques of the exorcism. In the same way, the titles attributed to Jesus by the sick people who approached him show no sign of the active intervention of the evangelist. They vary greatly, and there is no apparent reason why they should be uttered by any particular individual: 'Holy One of God' (1.24), 'Teacher' (4.38; 9.17), 'Sir' (7.28), 'Son of David' (10.48), 'Rabbouni' (10.51). It would be absurd to imagine that they had been introduced by the evangelist to bring about the triumph of a particular christology. And it is even less likely that Mark was trying to reduce these stories to a single type, to judge by the considerable diversity in the style of the miracle stories. In short, the active intervention of the evangelist seems to have been limited to the introductions and conclusions of the pericopae concerning the miracles, and to the redaction of generalizing summaries.

Apart from this, Mark's miracle stories are more or less identical with the documents which he used. Bultmann does not hesitate to say that they are Hellenistic in origin, for he finds in them the figure of the 'divine man' which is characteristic of the Greek literature of which the *Life of Apollonius of Tyana* by Philostratus, towards AD 300, was to be the most developed example.[5] He does recognize the existence of a certain number of Palestinian features in many of these narratives, beginning with the apophthegms which include an account of a miracle. But in his view most of the narratives remain Hellenistic. Bultmann has been followed in this view by many New Testament scholars, who are embarrassed by the narratives and who believe that they can dispense with them by attributing to them as remote and late an origin as possible. On one point their arguments go beyond those of their leader: they believe that behind the synoptic gospels, as behind the miracles of the Fourth Gospel, they can detect a written source composed of a series of miracle stories exalting the supernatural powers of a semi-divine being, an 'aretalogy'.[6]

We shall not enter here into a technical discussion on this hypothesis, which takes us back to the golden age of the criticism that existed before the *History of the Synoptic Tradition*. Let us say only that the very existence of a literary category of 'aretalogy' is seriously doubted by many reputable scholars of Graeco-Roman antiquity, at least in so far as an 'aretalogy' is supposed to consist of a series of miracle stories. There is no known example, and the 'aretalogists' who are occasionally mentioned are an ill-defined category of persons whom there is no reason to suppose to have had any vocation for literature. Even if one quotes the example of the 'signs source', the presence of which has often been postulated behind the miracle stories of the Fourth Gospel, this is far from establishing the existence of Hellenistic collections of narratives of this kind. In fact this 'signs source' is completely without substance. The arguments that are advanced on its behalf are weak. John 20.30f. is clearly a redactional passage; while the numbering of the signs (2.11; 4.51), which some scholars would regard as a trace of the source which conflicts with the context into which the evangelist has placed it, seems to us to be nothing more than a particular emphasis by the author on the small number of miracles carried out *in Galilee*, which he regarded as a place where virtually nothing important happened. As there is no difference in style between the miracle stories and the rest of the Fourth Gospel, and no particular unity amongst these narratives themselves, it is better to give up the idea of a written source and to admit with C. H. Dodd that the evangelist used isolated oral traditions comparable to those used by Mark.[7]

There remains Bultmann's statement that one can use the Hellenistic features and Palestinian aspects of the narratives to reconstruct a history of these traditions.[8] However attractive this thesis may be, it is necessary once again to insist that such a history is beyond our reach. In our view, all that can be done is to identify the setting in which these narratives were formed and handed down. Thus, for example, it is impossible to say that what is Palestinian is ancient and what is Hellenistic is more recent, once one realizes how far Hellenism had penetrated Palestine, particularly in frontier regions with a mixed population, like the district surrounding Lake Tiberias. In fact what is striking in the gospel miracle narratives is the mixture of Hellenistic and Judaeo-Palestinian features.[9] Such a mixture is conceivable only in a part of Palestine in which Judaism was in intimate contact with Hellenistic civilization, and only in a setting in which the dividing line between the two had more or less disappeared.

This does not apply to the conflict dialogues in which a miracle by Jesus forms the start of the argument. We have given a list of such texts above, pp. 51f. The original setting is in this case quite obviously Jewish, Palestinian, Rabbinic and Christian, and it is impossible to distinguish episodes which are later inventions from others. Matt. 17.24–27 and Luke 17.11–19, in which the miracle introduces a saying by Jesus, are closer to pure miracle stories. In the case of the latter, it is possible to identify the original setting only if one abandons the attempt to find it within the Christian church, where there was no room for Jesus as a village healer (Mark 7.31–37; 8.22–26) or Jesus as a magician (Mark 5.1–20; 11.12–14, 20–22), as he appears in a number of texts. As Bultmann himself quite rightly says, we need to ask how stories of this kind *found their way into* the gospel tradition.[10] But contrary to what the great scholar is only too ready to admit, this penetration did not take place until the moment of the redaction of the Gospel of Mark, or, in the case of a handful of narratives absent from Mark, during the years which followed this great literary event. We have no reason to suppose that the first-generation Christian church, which was on the defensive against Jewish attacks on the miracle-working gift of Jesus (cf. Mark 3.22–30 par.; Matt. 4.1–11 par.), used miracle stories other than those included in the controversies described above. It required the passionate interest of the evangelist Mark, and later the moderating effect of the passage of time, for these narratives to become the object of meditation and theological reflection.

If the setting in which the miracle stories originated and were handed down for a time is not a Christian one, but must be sought in the region of Palestine into which Hellenism had penetrated in a popular and superstitious form, the obvious place to look is the village society of north-eastern Galilee or the area immediately surrounding Lake Tiberias. Story-tellers at markets and during the winter evenings found a ready audience for narratives with no literary pretensions, but too sensational to leave a popular audience unmoved. The name of Jesus had not been forgotten in this region where he had done so much work, particularly in the small towns and villages (Mark 1.38–45; 8.27). His work as an exorcist and healer was remembered. People were diverted and encouraged by recalling the mighty acts he had performed at no great distance from the place where they lived. The evangelist Mark, inspired by a lively concern for the multitude and critical of the church of Jerusalem, which he considered dormant, saw the value of such documents to him in order to break the monopoly of the church tradition and its portrait of Jesus. We owe to him the introduction of these narratives into a Christian setting.

As for the 'signs' of the Fourth Gospel, their original setting must have been much the same, even if it is less easy to locate it geographically. The village society of Galilee could have supplied the story of the wedding at Cana (John 2.1–11), of the son of the royal official (4.46–54), and perhaps also those of the feeding of the multitude and the walking on the water (6.1–15 and 6.16–21), in so far as the Fourth Gospel, in these three last cases, is not using adaptations of the parallel stories in the synoptic gospels (Matt. 8.5–13 par.; Mark 6.35–44 par.; Mark 8.1–10 par.; Mark 6.45–52 par.). As for the healings in chapters 5 and 9, and the raising of Lazarus (John 11.1ff.), a Judaean setting cannot be excluded. But it is difficult to be more exact, since the redactional activity of the evangelist has obscured the outlines of the original documents. In any case, two generations had passed before they were used, and this delay may have brought with it even further modifications.

Popular story-tellers have always had an extraordinary memory. Thus although the tradition of miracle stories may not have had the systematic character of that of the dominical sayings, this does not mean that it lacks fidelity. In the form in which they occur in the Gospel of Mark, one may suppose that the original narratives are to be found almost unchanged, except with regard to their introductions and conclusions. But of course this does not resolve the problem of the historicity of the events they recount, any more than it excludes the introduction into the tradition concerning Jesus of narratives derived from folk-lore or of episodes borrowed from one or other of the cycles of legends recounting the mighty acts of a famous person of the past (Moses, Elijah, etc.). But it is impossible to say with certainty whether any particular story is borrowed, and that another is historical. Once again, the available criteria are completely subjective and unconvincing. Why should a narrative be dismissed because it is 'unedifying'? Why should one suppose that it goes back to the origin of the tradition because it emphasizes the mercifulness of Jesus? Nothing could be less obvious than this should be so, since this tradition has nothing to do with the Christian church.

Thus we are led once again to consider the gospel miracle stories as a whole, and to limit our inquiry to the portrait of Jesus which is found in them all. Obviously this portrait does not conform to our modern standards and shows us only one side of Jesus. But it does so in a fairly reliable way, for those who heard these stories had themselves seen and heard the hero of them all, and would not have accepted a presentation which was incompatible with their own recollections. The portrait of the Master that the story-tellers presented to their public is indeed the one retained by the multitudes who had met Jesus. Thus it gives us a point of view about the historical Jesus which it would be very wrong to neglect, because it provides a useful complement to the portrait drawn by the disciples, and that outlined in their turn by his middle-class hearers.

The most obvious feature of the portrait of Jesus which we find in the miracle stories is his extraordinary power. Even though the author of the Fourth Gospel considered the synoptic miracle stories somewhat slight, to read them is nevertheless to receive a striking impression of power. The Master seems to be a man like any other – and suddenly a gesture or a word displays his divine authority over the elements (Mark 4.35–41 par.; 6.35–44 par.; 6.45–52 par.; 8.1–10 par.; 11.12–14, 20–22; John 2.1–11). He is an outstanding example of the 'divine man' as conceived by popular Hellenism, but he is also the emissary of God like Moses and the prophets. One cannot speak of a christology of the miracle stories, for there is no attempt at reflection behind the fearful statement of the immense power of Jesus. Mark is the first to make this attempt, in seeking to go beyond the christology of the dominical sayings, as has been well demonstrated by Kenzo Tagawa in *Miracles et Evangile: la pensée personelle de l'évangeliste Marc*.[11]

This power, usually concealed, which was no doubt thought of as acting without any spectacular display and as protecting the disciples, was sometimes manifested in an almost accidental fashion, when Jesus was being buffeted by the crowd (Mark 5.25–34 par.) or taken by surprise as he slept (Mark 4.35–41 par.), or obliged to accept his responsibilities to an unreasonable multitude (Mark 6.35–44 par.; 8.1–10 par.). It was not un-limited, for the demons were able to resist him to some extent (Mark 5.1–20 par.); and the ailment was not always overcome without effort (Mark 8.22–26); but it far exceeded that of the disciples (Mark 9.14–29 par.); and Jesus used words with an almost creative effectiveness (Mark 4.39 par.; 5.41 par.). He had a special relationship with the demonic powers, who recog-nized his authority, but regarded his presence as an aggression (Mark 1.23f. par.; 5.7ff. par.; 9.20, 25). This is as much as to say that he belonged to the world on high, from which they had been excluded.

This semi-divine being used his immense power principally in order to heal the sick. One can perceive in these stories the longing of a whole people who had no access to medicine, and amongst whom disease was constantly present in every form. Again, one can perceive the extraordinary reputation achieved by the activities of a healer who at last was successful. Jesus could do almost anything against sickness – the remark in Mark 6.5f. does not occur in a miracle story! But what makes his personality even more exceptional is that he was merciful and dealt without payment with all the cases brought to him. This disinterestedness sometimes led him to prevent, as far as possible, the story of a healing spreading (1.44; 5.43; 7.36; 8.26?). It also prevented him from staying in one place to carry out his work there for some time.

Thus the opportunity, always fleeting, had to be seized when it offered. Jesus did not take the initiative. He consented to act when he was sought out, or reacted to an attack or to a necessity. Thus those who heard these stories became aware of a certain reluctance on the part of the Master to play the role of a healer. They perceived that his true mission was elsewhere. But they knew that he was moved by anyone who trusted him (Mark 5.25–34; Matt. 8.5–13 par.), and was ready to hold back the moment he perceived doubt (Mark 9.14–30 par.).

This Jesus was a lonely person. The disciples who sometimes surrounded him are presented in a poor light, as persons who had little understanding of him and very limited powers of their own (Mark 5.31f.; 6.35f.; 8.4; 9.14ff.). They are present nevertheless, as if the Galilean story-tellers knew that there existed in their own time a Christian church claiming a monopoly of the risen Jesus, and were rather amused at this situation.

The image of the Master which is to be found in these miracle stories is strange not only to us as modern men, but also to an orthodox Jew or an educated Greek of the first century of our era. How can one believe that this sympathetic but rather disturbing magician is the same as the Master of the dominical sayings and the skilled narrator of parables? Should not such doubtful evidence be resolutely ignored, and the historical Jesus reconstructed in isolation from it? This has often been done in the past, and is a temptation to anyone who sets out to give an account of the teaching of Jesus but neglects activities of a different kind attributed to him in the gospels.[12]

But to eliminate what disturbs us in the documentary evidence is a procedure open to suspicion from the start. The dominical sayings and the conflict dialogues bear witness to the fact that the miracle working of Jesus was known, discussed and defended by the church from the very first generation (Mark 3.22ff. par.; Matt. 4.1ff. par.; etc.). Thus this activity belongs to the sphere of history, even if every one of the miracle stories must be regarded as improbable. Good historical method drives us to an inquiry into the significance of the existence of such stories for the knowledge of the historical Jesus.

The first thing this fact signifies is that he aroused interest and sympathy amongst the simplest people of the Galilean countryside. Not enough has been said about the importance of this phenomenon, which is quite unusual in a society in which the religious exclusiveness of all the active movements (Pharisees, Essenes and even Zealots) seems to have resulted in the increasing alienation of the mass of the people. Jesus, even more than John the Baptist, concerned himself with the multitude, and found the way to their hearts. While his preaching of the grace of God for all enabled him to do this, it was due in the first instance to his activity as a healer, which responded to a social need well known in societies in which medicine was the prerogative of a few privileged persons.

There is more than this in the miracle stories. As we have said, Jesus is presented in them as a mysterious person capable of communicating with the world on high, and drawing on a power which goes beyond that of the most gifted man. In our view, it is not arbitrary to see in this the popular equivalent of the recognition by the disciples of the very special authority which radiated from his person. In a somewhat naïvely mythological language, it is an interesting confirmation of the portrait of Jesus which we find in the dominical sayings. The very fact that people who were ready to use this language spoke of the healer of Nazareth in terms which recall those used by the disciples indicates that the authority of the Master went beyond the classical categories of Jewish Messianism and Hellenistic ideologies.

The miracle stories show us a Jesus who was sometimes reticent, who was not always prepared to do what was asked of him, and who in any case hardly ever took the initiative in miraculous healings. Is this a sign that the Master was not at his ease in this somewhat ambiguous role? We shall never know for certain. What is certain is that Jesus reacted vigorously against the accusations of magic made against him (Mark 3.22ff. par.), and that he had to take care not to lay himself open to them by allowing the desires of the crowd to persuade him to go too far. But there is no reason to suppose that he did not accept his role as a healer as one of the elements in the mission God had entrusted to him. Even if this led to the spread of stories and representations of his person with which he could not have been wholly in agreement, he seems to have decided to run these risks in order not to cut himself off from the mass of the people, to whom he knew he had been sent (Luke 13.31–33).

Thus we cannot simply reject the image of a more or less divine magician which we find in the miracle stories. For these brief narratives do in fact put us in touch with a dimension of the historical Jesus.

8

Jesus as a Public Figure

As we have seen, all the strata of oral tradition have come to us by way of particular and limited groups. In the case of the dominical sayings, this is obvious. The parables take us back to a social class which was comparatively few in number. In the case of the miracle stories, the circle grows larger, but even here it hardly extends beyond the people of the Galilean country-side, and probably of a very small part of Galilee. Nowhere does Jesus appear as a true public figure, for example on the scale of the Jewish nation of Palestine. He remains a provincial prophet, without any apparent hold over the majority of the population of the country.

This being so, how can one explain his condemnation by the highest courts and his execution by the Romans at Jerusalem? What is the explanation of the relentless determination of certain high-ranking dignitaries at Jerusalem to destroy someone who was so small a threat to them? It is difficult to attribute this to an accident or an unfortunate chance. Thus something must have happened which made the local preacher of Galilee into a nationally known figure with sufficient influence to disturb the Jewish and Roman authorities. It cannot, of course, have been a very important event, otherwise it would have left some trace in the work of the Jewish historian Flavius Josephus or in the Greek and Roman historians of the period, and this is not the case. But something must have happened.

The gospels tell us, before the Passion narrative, of a number of scenes situated at Jerusalem, mostly in the Temple or not far from it; that is, in the place where a bold statement or gesture would be likely to attract the most attention, especially during the great Jewish festivals, which drew to the sanctuary crowds of pilgrims who had sometimes travelled a great distance. It is amongst these episodes that we must look for the incident (or incidents) which could have brought Jesus sufficient national influence to provoke a defensive reaction amongst the established authorities. Since the location of many of them is uncertain (cf. for example the controversies in Mark 11 and 12 par.), and since a straightforward sermon uttered on some occasion in the midst of the immense crowd gathered in the Temple court could not possibly have been heard by any great number, there are only two episodes which can be considered: the entry into Jerusalem and the driving out of the merchants from the Temple.

The solemn entry of the Master into Jerusalem (Mark 11.1–10 par.) is regarded by some critics as having formed a comparatively impressive Messianic demonstration, and for this reason as having alarmed those who were responsible for keeping order. But the gospel narrative, beginning with the considerably edited version of the tradition given by Mark (cf. above, p. 63), is not very explicit. The Messianic nature of the acclamations, which is obvious in the other three evangelists, is much less so in the Gospel of Mark, where Jesus does not receive the title 'king', and where the demonstration is above all a kind of 'pilgrim liturgy' very close to what seems to have been the practice every year at Jerusalem.[1] Since Mark himself had gone a long way towards putting more weight on the part played by Jesus, by introducing the episode of the search for the ass, one must wonder whether the tradition was doing anything more than handing down a hymn taught by Jesus to his disciples, with the intention that it should be sung every time the group entered any town, bringing the kingdom of God with it. This hymn may also have been used in the later Christian liturgy. Thus it would not be prudent to read this narrative as a report of an episode which sealed the fate of the Master by giving him a widespread hold on public opinion.

All that remains, then, is the story of the driving out of the merchants from the Temple (Mark 11.15ff. par.), which many critics regard as fictional.[2] I have argued in great detail elsewhere[3] why the apophthegm which recounts this episode can be regarded as forming part of the oldest church tradition, and what practical use was made of it in the primitive church of Jerusalem. I have also shown that the use of it by the Christian community in the Jewish capital only a few years after the events took place is a guarantee of the historicity of the episode. Its importance should not be exaggerated, but it had very great consequences for Jesus. I shall do no more here than summarize a few points in the argument.

Critics who, like Robert Eisler[4] and S. G. F. Brandon,[5] turn this incident in the Temple into a large-scale military operation, are obliged to assume that Jesus acted as the leader of a secret army, or that he held 'Zealot' convictions which are incompatible with all the rest of the gospel tradition. Since in any case the narrative of the driving out of the merchants from the Temple is a very slight basis for the reconstruction of a pitched battle, it is difficult to find grounds for a thesis of this kind. It may at least serve to remind us of a fact which is often too much ignored, that is, that the Jerusalem Temple was an immense administrative unit, guarded by a powerful body of police. Every event which took place in this setting was very soon known throughout the country, especially if it happened at the time when there was a great influx of pilgrims, during the great feasts, which drew as many as a hundred thousand people from outside into a town which usually had many fewer inhabitants than this. In this way, Jesus' action towards the merchants, a very rapid action with no further consequences, may have taken on the dimensions of a great event in Jewish opinion. The merchants, whose presence in the Temple was the object of lively discussion on more than one occasion before AD 70, and whose prices must often have been found excessive by the pilgrims, were certainly unpopular, even if they were needed. The authorities who ran the Temple, and particularly the high priest, were suspected of collusion with the Roman occupiers, and their financial power brought them many criticisms, concluding dramatically with the internal struggles during the war of AD 66–70. To learn that these people had been defeated or had suffered a setback on their own ground must have caused great enthusiasm amongst many pilgrims, and subsequently amongst a good proportion of the Jews of Palestine.

In a few minutes, Jesus had become a public figure. Henceforth, his sayings and actions were of interest not merely to a few limited groups who had been in direct contact with him. He provoked comment and reactions in the masses of the people, even if they had no personal contact with him. His popularity was no doubt fleeting and remained a matter of dispute. But it was both a widespread and a very sudden popularity, and its potential political significance could not but be obvious to all who retained some little power in the Palestine of that time.

The synoptic gospels do not leave time for the popularity which the Master acquired in the Temple court to bear fruit. Only a few days after the driving out of the merchants, Jesus is arrested and executed, as if his action had sparked off the explosion. This interpretation of the facts is accepted by the great majority of biographers of Jesus, who seem to regard it as the obvious course of events. However, the Fourth Gospel places the events in a quite different order, locating the driving out of the merchants at the beginning of Jesus' public ministry. Moreover, the passion narratives contain no allusion to this episode, and this makes it difficult to see how it could have been the immediate cause of his condemnation. One might also suppose that the political accusations made against Jesus in order to have him put to death by the Romans would have seemed improbable if they had been based only on the minor incident in the Temple taken on its own.

This casts doubt, we consider, on the chronology of the synoptic gospels, which is as arbitrary on this point as on all others, and has no basis in the pre-gospel tradition. The evangelist Mark, followed by Matthew and Luke, decided for literary and theological reasons to place at the end of his book all scenes located at Jerusalem. It has often been pointed out (M. Goguel, T. W. Manson, etc.) that this editorial presentation is very unlikely from a historical point of view. Jesus probably made several visits to Jerusalem (Matt. 23.37–39 par.) as a pilgrim on the occasion of festivals, and since the driving out of the merchants from the Temple played no part in his trial, it took place during a pilgrimage which was not that of his last Passover.

It is not possible to be more exact. A few weeks or a few months before his arrest, Jesus suddenly achieved great notoriety. This violent entry on to the public scene caused jealousy and opposition, especially in the ruling circles, both Jewish and Roman. The personal situation of Jesus (who, it was feared, might bring the people into revolt against the priestly oligarchy and its foreign protectors) must have become dangerous almost at once, especially in the regions to which the authority of the Jerusalem Sanhedrin and the Roman prefect extended.

The dangers were all the greater because of the way in which certain sayings of the Master were interpreted and distorted by the multitude, as well as by his opponents. There is in the pre-gospel tradition a striking example of this phenomenon: the fate of the declaration by Jesus concerning the destruction and rebuilding of the Temple, a statement which the driving out of the merchants brought into particular prominence. According to Mark 14.56–59 and Matt. 26.60f., some false witnesses testified before the Sanhedrin which met to judge Jesus, that he had proclaimed that he would destroy the Temple and rebuild it in three days. Mark hastens to add that their testimony did not agree, 'not even so' – an odd remark, which Matthew suppressed, not knowing what to make of it. It suggests that unlike the other accusations, there was some substance in this. In fact the two evangelists do give a saying of Jesus concerning the *destruction* of the Temple (Mark 13.1f. and Matt, 24.1f.). But in their view this is his only declaration on the subject, and it mentions neither any part played by Jesus in the ruin of the sanctuary, nor any rebuilding.

The evangelist Luke does not mention the false witnesses in his version of the trial of Jesus, thus eliminating any reference to any distortion of a saying concerning the destruction of the Temple. But the same writer tells us that Stephen was accused of having foretold the destruction of the Temple by his Master (Acts 6.13f.). Whatever the origin of this statement may be, it suggests the existence of a more drastic version of the prophecy of the ruin of the sanctuary, of which Luke 21.5f. gives the usual version, similar to that in Mark 13 and Matthew 24. Moreover, in his speech (Acts 7.44ff.) Stephen shows such a lively hostility towards the Jerusalem Temple that in spite of the falseness of the charges made against him (Acts 6.13), one may ask whether in fact he did not use this strengthened version of the dominical saying concerning the destruction of the sanctuary. One would then have to accept that it was perhaps not a deliberate falsification, but rather one of the forms taken by an utterance which had widespread currency amongst many groups and in many places, where it could hardly be checked.

The Fourth Gospel confirms this hypothesis. In John 2.19, Jesus declares in the discussion which follows the scene of the driving out of the merchants that in three days he would rebuild the Temple, when the 'Jews' had destroyed it. This saying is closer to the statement made by the false witnesses in Mark and Matthew, in that it adds to the theme of the destruction of the Temple that of its rebuilding by Jesus. Even if John to some extent recast it (he interpreted it in his own way in any case: John 2.20f.), it may well be a more accurate version of the original statement by Jesus.

In any case, this statement was clearly not handed down in an organized and sure way. The prophecy of the ruin of the Temple seems to have found a place in the tradition of apophthegms, so that its form remained strongly fixed. But the declaration in which the rebuilding of the Temple by Jesus was mentioned must have circulated very widely amongst the Jews after the sensational driving out of the merchants. This explains the variations in it and the different interpretations, sometimes hostile and sometimes favourable, which it received. For the opponents of Jesus, a saying of this kind would confirm that he was indeed the dangerous agitator that his actions indicated. In the eyes of the multitude, it meant that there was something Messianic or prophetic about his person.

There are a number of indications in the gospels of this enthusiastic attitude to Jesus on the part of the multitude. Of course many of these indications are due to the redactors, since the evangelists had a tendency to stress the success which the Master achieved. In particular, we have shown that one cannot give too great credence to the narrative of the solemn entry into Jerusalem, especially since it echoes scenes which were no doubt repeated when he entered many places (cf. above p. 111). But a fair number of the episodes which come from the church tradition or from popular recollection bear witness to the great popularity of Jesus at some period in his ministry. It is quite likely that some of them date back to the period after the episode in the Temple.

The story of the healing of the blind man of Jericho (Mark 10.45–52 par.) and the Zacchaeus episode (Luke 19.1–10) both assume the presence of a great multitude, and deep feelings of enthusiasm for the Master on the part of people who had never met him. Whatever the history of their transmission, the historical event to which they go back may well have taken place after Jesus had achieved the status of a public figure, so far as we can tell from the attitude of the heroes of these two episodes towards the Master, who is regarded by the first as 'Son of David' and accepted by the second as a judge.

The same may be said of the two stories of the feeding of the multitude (Mark 6.35–45 par.; 8.1–10 par.; John 6.1ff.). This episode is conceivable during the period before the driving out of the merchants, but should rather be dated after this incident, in the order given in the Fourth Gospel, on account of the enormous crowd it implies.

The narrative of Peter's confession at Caesarea Philippi (Mark 8.27ff. par.) assumes that there was considerable discussion amongst the Jewish people of Palestine concerning the mission committed to Jesus by God. His identification with John the Baptist can easily be conceived of during the provincial period of his career. But it is more easily understood after his confrontation with the authorities at Jerusalem, since the Baptist achieved notoriety through his conflict with Antipas (Mark 6.17ff. par.; Josephus, *Antiquities of the Jews*, XVIII, 5, 2). As for the other indentifications proposed by the multitude for Jesus, either that of 'one of the prophets' or 'Elijah', there is every likelihood that they date from after the Temple incident, which could very easily bear comparison with episodes in the life of the prophets in which they came forward to purify the cult (cf. I Kings 18.20ff.; Amos, passim; Jeremiah 7).

It is likely that this popular enthusiasm led some people to the conclusion that Jesus was the expected Messiah. Of course, at Caesarea Philippi this opinion was expressed by the disciples alone (Mark 8.29 par.), but the very concise style of the narrative suggests that they were taking up an idea which had already been uttered by others. The allusions to David which are found here and there in appeals addressed to Jesus (Mark 10.45–52 par.; 11.10 par.), the question by the high priest during the trial (Mark 14.61 par.), and above all the condemnation by the Romans and the execution of Jesus by crucifixion with the sign 'King of the Jews' on the cross, are convincing evidence that many people identified Jesus with the Messiah. A movement of public opinion of this kind is conceivable only after the driving out of the merchants.

One may add that the pressure exercised by the crowd during the course of the trial of Jesus and its preliminaries, even if it had been exaggerated by Christian writers, seems to have been real: the hurried arrest at night, the expeditious procedure and the immediate execution are easier to explain if the Jewish and Roman authorities wanted to prevent Jesus from stirring up the crowd of Passover pilgrims, and at the same time to prevent mass movements in favour of a very popular prisoner. These two dangers existed only in so far as Jesus was regarded as Messiah by a sufficiently large proportion of the people.

This wave of enthusiasm may have been brief, but it may well have seemed a menace to the established order, like many others in the first century of our era. Those in authority responded to it by threats and then by violence. The pre-gospel tradition also preserves some traces of this reaction, especially where Jesus is shown as being harried, spied upon or ready to sacrifice his life. Certain forms of opposition, which may have been present before Jesus achieved notoriety, seem more probable after this decisive turning point. Thus for example the violent confrontation in the affair of the man with the withered hand (Mark 3.1–6 par.) presupposes a high degree of tension between Jesus and opponents determined to harm him by making use of the slightest slip on his part. Similarly, the dispute concerning the origin of Jesus' power to exorcize (Mark 3.22ff. par.) is comprehensible only if the Jewish authorities were looking for grounds for an accusation which would allow them to get rid of this dangerous agitator. And again, the Master's brutal attack on the 'tradition of men' (Mark 7.1–13 par.) is explicable only if the criticisms made against the disciples about their neglect of ritual purity were traps set by ruthless opponents.

It is even more probable that sayings in which Jesus describes himself as wandering and threatened should be dated after the driving out of the merchants from the Temple: Mark 2.19f. par.; 10.38–45 par.; Matt. 8.19f. par.; 23.37–39; Luke 12.49f.; 13.31–33; 17.22–25; 22.35–38. Here, too, one may mention the prophecies of the Passion in Mark 8.31 par.; 9.31

par.; 10.32–34 par. Many passages where the disciples are exhorted to total sacrifice of their goods and their property may perhaps also go back to this glorious but difficult period in the life of the Master: Mark 8.34ff. par.; 10.29f. par.; Matt. 5.10–12; 10.17–39 par.

In short, there is no lack of evidence in the synoptic gospels to confirm the hypothesis set out above, even though it cannot be based upon the existence of a stratum of tradition representing the point of view of the great mass of the Jewish population of Palestine about the person of Jesus. The prophet of Nazareth, involuntarily drawn into the foreground of public attention, no doubt occupied this position for no more than a few weeks or a few months, before succumbing to the blows of the alliance which had formed against him as his popularity grew, following the affair in the Temple. But this brief period was very important in many respects.

In particular, it posed the question of the attitude that Jesus adopted towards political Messianism, the Zealot movement and the brigands who made it their business to right wrongs and seem to have infested certain remote regions of Palestine at that period. We do not know whether the Master had anything to do with these tendencies and groups before he caused the uproar in the Temple market. There is no certainty that these movements had their base in Galilee, contrary to the often repeated assertion; and the activity of the Zealots as an organized group underwent something of an eclipse during the period of John the Baptist, Jesus and the early Christians, to judge by the silence of the historian Josephus concerning them until about AD 50. In his own way, Jesus may have been inspired by a kind of Zealot ideology of direct action in defence of the honour of God when he took action to rid the outer court of the Temple of the permanent market which had established itself there: the example of Phineas (Num. 25.1–15), kept alive by that of Mattathias (I Maccabees 2.15–28), may have provoked him to take into his own hands the task which the authorities no longer carried out, that of the punishment of those who profaned God; this is what the Zealots did themselves,[6] they too being inspired by these heroes of the past. But this must remain conjectural.

On the other hand, it is more or less certain that once he was seized by the whirlwind of widespread popularity, Jesus was rapidly brought face to face with movements admired or feared by the whole Jewish population of Palestine. Towards the political Messianism which is expressed, for example, in the seventeenth *Psalm of Solomon*, and which is in accordance with the simple aspirations of the masses, he does not seem to have adopted as negative an attitude as that attributed to him by Jean Héring,[7] on the basis of his replies to the high priest during his trial (Mark 14.61f. par.) and to Peter after the confession at Caesarea Philippi (Mark 8.30ff.). In passages less visibly edited than these, such as the conclusion of the feeding of the multitude (Mark 6.45 par.; 8.9ff. par.; John 6.14ff.), we have rather a refusal to commit himself too completely, and the same is true of acts full of symbolic meaning such as the choice of an ass as his mount for the solemn entry into Jerusalem or into other places (Mark 11.1ff. par.), which is an obvious reference to the prophecy of Zechariah 9.9f.

Jesus' striking action in the Temple must have won him some sympathy in the Zealot movement. It may be that the adherence of Zealots to the group of his disciples was the consequence of this act. We know that at least one of the Twelve was called 'the Cananaean' (Mark 3.18; Matt. 10.4) or the 'Zealot' (Luke 6.15; Acts 1.13): both words mean the same. It may also be that the surnames of Judas Iscariot and Simon Bar-Jona signify '*sicarius*' and 'anarchist' (R. Eisler), which would make them either Zealots or sympathizers with them. Jesus did not try to reject this compromising support. But his teaching about the law and the kingdom of God is so different from what we know of Zealot doctrine that it was impossible to confuse the two.

As for the brigands who lived the life of outlaws and enjoyed a certain amount of popular prestige, to the extent that it is difficult to distinguish between them and the claimants to the title of Messiah who arose from time to time, Jesus does not seem to have had any dealings with them, unless Judas Iscariot or Simon Bar-Jona came from their ranks, which is questionable. On the other hand, it is probable that he himself was considered as a kind of nationalist brigand by the Romans: the episode of Barabbas and his crucifixion between two bandits confirms at least that this was the meaning of his condemnation as 'King of the Jews' in the eyes of the Roman authorities.

According to a tradition peculiar to Luke, and close to that of the apophthegms, Jesus did in fact do enough to make this identification possible. The dialogue of Luke 22.35–38 must be understood as follows: by making sure that his disciples had at least a minimum of arms, the Master made a Roman trial inevitable, especially after the brief struggle in Gethsemane (Mark 14.47–50 par.). Was he attempting, by so doing, to avoid falling under the jurisdiction of the Sanhedrin? This is not out of the question.

Thus Jesus, exposed as a public figure to all the misunderstandings and pressures of public opinion, neither withdrew from the current which was carrying him with it, nor allowed himself to be carried away completely by it. He accepted the immense popularity which the affair in the Temple brought him, up to and including the Messianic interpretation of his person and his work. But at the same time he kept his distance with regard to the role that people wanted him to play: Messiah, but in his own way; associated with the Zealots, but differing completely from them by his behaviour and his inspiration; ready to be identified with the brigands, but refusing to act with them in the same way.

This attitude of cautious consent towards the image that the multitudes of Palestine had of him is to some extent similar to the way in which he reacted to the conception of him held by the various groups with which he had been connected previously. This faces us with the final question, which cannot be evaded, even if we do not know how to answer it. This Jesus, this man of many faces, who was he?

9

Who was Jesus?

Looking at the very different portraits of the person and work of Jesus that we find in the pre-gospel tradition, we might be tempted to choose one or the other, as many of his biographers do, explicitly or implicitly. For some, what matters is the political-religious Messiah acclaimed by the mass of the Jewish people of Palestine after the driving out of the merchants from the Temple; for others, the ingenious moralist of the parables, the favourite of the lower-middle and middle class; for others, the prophet of the kingdom of God which is mysteriously present, whose preaching brought liberty, as the disciples knew him; for others again, the semi-divine magician, ready to help everyone, who was never forgotten by the peasants of north-eastern Galilee. There are even writers who regard Jesus as virtually nothing more than the martyr whose death brings the certainty of salvation to those who meditate upon it; they are interested only in the central figure of the Passion narrative.

The virtue of a choice of this kind is that it makes Jesus easily comprehensible. Nothing is more simple, once a person is reduced to one main dimension, than to admire him unreservedly or to reject him completely, depending upon one's taste. Nothing is easier than to present one's time, or one's chosen audience, with an up-to-date Christ from whom all complexity has been removed.

However, after the discovery of the many and various portraits of Jesus with which the tradition provides us, such an over-simplification is clearly so arbitrary that we should hardly be expected to do other than dismiss it. It is indispensable to integrate the complexity of Jesus' personality into an attempt at a synthesis which can give it the coherence without which it is incomprehensible to the human mind.

Many of the biographers of Jesus have thought it possible to do this by reconstructing the Master's own consciousness of himself and his mission, and particularly his 'Messianic consciousness'. Innumerable essays have been written which have striven to demonstrate either positively, why, how, and from what moment Jesus understood himself as the Messiah, the Son of God or the Son of man – or, negatively, never considered himself as anything other than a wise man, a rabbi or a prophet. Writers of this kind have become more cautious since the development of the form-critical method, but we have not seen the last of it. Scholars assert almost as boldly as in the past[1] that if Jesus could show himself in such various lights, it was because he knew (or did not know) that he was the Messiah, the Son of God or the Son of man. Some think that the Master spoke and acted as Messiah wherever he went: for the disciples he was the reformer of the law and the supreme eschatological messenger; for those who heard his parables he was preaching about himself; for the multitude in Galilee he was the Son of God with magical powers; but in each case all he wanted was to impose his own conception of Messiahship. Others, however, consider that Jesus never acted as Messiah and never said anything about himself, and that everything which gives the contrary impression is the post-resurrection creation of the Christian church.

We find it difficult to imagine where so many eminent scholars derive the certainty with which they defend these contradictory theses. Even if we allow that the pre-gospel tradition can be distinguished in its entirety from the redactional elements which surround it in the gospels, the absence of any serious criterion for sifting what is primitive from what is secondary in this tradition presents, as we have pointed out, a major difficulty in any historical inquiry. In these circumstances, what hope can there be of penetrating to the most profound and most personal motivations of a being as different from us as Jesus, whatever one's view of his divinity and his messiahship? It is astonishing to see so many people flying in the face of this obvious fact.

In order to achieve, as far as possible, a synthesis which will make Jesus comprehensible, we believe that a different way must be sought. A comparison must be made between the attitudes taken by Jesus to the various ideas people had of his person. If this comparison were to show that there were certain constant features in these attitudes, it might provide a key to his behaviour.

The first constant factor which strikes us is that each of the portraits of Jesus is the result of an initiative on his part. That formed by the disciples is a straightforward response to the preaching of the kingdom of God and the appeal made to particular people to come and help Jesus in his task. The image which the Passion narratives convey to us in strongly influenced by the initiative Jesus took at his last meal with his disciples, a prophetic act which sealed the fate of the Master and suggested a soteriological interpretation of the cross. The portrait of the healer of Nazareth which was cherished in the Galilean countryside was a product of the miracle-working acts on which Jesus ventured when sick persons hampered his preaching work. The portrait reflected in the parables results from Jesus' choosing the role of storyteller towards middle-class groups. As for the image of Jesus as a public figure, it derives in its entirety from the most aggressive of the initiatives which the Master took: the driving out of the merchants from the Temple.

We need not go into more detail. Whatever qualifications one might wish to add to this statement, the fact is that Jesus was able to take the initiatives needed to give an impression of himself very different from that which would have been suggested by his origin (Mark 6.1–6 par.) or by current ideas (Mark 2.17 par.; 10.35–45 par.; Matt. 10.34–36 par.). We find in Jesus neither a submission to the current patterns of thought which could have been applied to him, nor a retreat into an ivory tower, but rather a firm will to assert himself publicly towards particular human groups.

The second constant feature that can be observed in the attitude of Jesus with regard to the various portraits of himself which were current is the extraordinary zest which enabled this humble figure to give such unusual depth to these portraits. In the eyes of his astonished disciples, the Master who taught them with familiar methods was distinguished from others by the novelty and boldness of his teaching, by the absolute nature of his appeal, and by the way he committed his hearers to action. For the peasants of Galilee he was a much more powerful and more generous healer than others of his kind. For the members of the middle classes, this storyteller and moralist was without equal, and they accepted from him criticisms which they would never have tolerated from anyone else. For the masses in Palestine, their enthusiasm aroused by his gesture at the Temple, he was much more than one Zealot or one brigand among others; he was the elect of God who would lead his people to their final liberation, if the boldness of his actions and the vigorousness of his eschatological preaching was any indication.

There can be no question that Jesus was exceptionally talented. The setting in which birth had placed him was a modest one, and the various fields of his activity – apart from the Jerusalem Temple, a centre of religion known throughout the civilized world of the Mediterranean basin and the Middle East – remained very humble. In spite of this, the impression produced by his personality and his activities soon spread far and wide. There are, of course, innumerable explanations for this, but it is due above all to his personal qualities. To neglect his personal presence and activity would be to condemn oneself to understand nothing of the history of Christian origins, which is completely dominated by this exceptional personality with almost unlimited talents.

A third constant feature which is of interest lies in the attitude of Jesus to the various conceptions people had of him: his more or less active acceptance of each of these conceptions. The Master was quite ready to play the part assigned to him by the disciples, the peasants of Galilee, the Palestinian middle class, and the great mass of the Jewish people. In each case, he played this part with some reserve, for fear of being swallowed up by one or other of these groups. But he did not refuse to play it; on the contrary. For some he was the Master, for others he was a storyteller, for others again a healer, and for the multitudes a Messianic personality. But he persevered in the activity which had obtained him each of these titles, apparently without attempting to make these various portraits compatible with each other, or to do much to put right what was unsatisfactory in them.

Thus one may say that Jesus brought into being, reinforced

and accepted all these portraits, however imperfect and difficult to reconcile with each other they may have been. Must we describe this as opportunism, as has sometimes been done with regard to Paul's making himelf 'all things to all men' (I Cor. 9.19–23)? In both cases this would be to forget that we are dealing with an eschatological preacher who is seeking to reach the largest possible number of people in a very short time. Like his apostle after him, Jesus wanted to do a lot very quickly. His whole behaviour is dominated by the desire to bring to the kingdom of God groups who were as different from each other as they could be. The person of the preacher is not so important as to justify stopping the spread of the gospel by dictating to his audience the terms to be used for describing Jesus.

However, as in the case of Paul, the authority of the one who was speaking in the name of God was essential to a balanced message. Nothing said or done in the sight of any of the groups whom Jesus encountered would have had much significance if he had not been marvelled at by those with whom he came into contact. Thus the portrait of the Master found in the tradition which derives from different groups reflects this unbreakable union between the work and its author. By accepting it in each case, Jesus showed that he claimed a very high authority, the highest that the group was prepared to accord to him. By not proposing any synthesis between these portraits, he suggested that none of them, and none of those which could be superimposed upon them, could do full justice to his person and his mission.

Thus the 'mystery of Jesus' is not a more or less artificial creation by later generations. It is rooted in the behaviour of Jesus himself, completely devoted to his humble task, but convinced that for this mission he possessed an exceptional authority from God; involved in several simultaneous dialogues and not trying to draw them into a unity; too great to be wholly understood by any of his interlocutors, but grasped in part by many of them. This mystery already necessitated the groping efforts of the evangelists and theologians of the first century. It has never been finally eliminated, either by historians or by theologians. It never will be.

No biographer will ever be able to do more than assemble the data for this mystery. Everyone must then attempt an intuitive and necessarily imperfect solution with the means which his time and place provide. The conception that the believer makes of Jesus with the aid of the doctrine of his church is as legitimate here as that which the unbeliever draws from the philosophy practised round about him. But it is not more legitimate.

Even if both are contradictory, they are no more so than the various portraits which we find in the pre-gospel tradition. We are not capable of making a synthesis of them, but we can maintain that whenever they are based on the texts and show a certain sympathy for Jesus, they represent legitimate points of view about the unique and elusive object that he is. A believer may consider that he has a unique relationship with Christ. He cannot make Jesus Christ his property or deny that the unbeliever may also be in contact with Jesus.

In short, the mystery of Jesus, now as ever, is that he can speak of God and man to very different groups, using for each the language which it is capable of understanding and obtaining acknowledgment of his authority from them all, even though it is expressed in such divergent terms that no synthesis is possible. The mystery of Jesus is that he is and remains the object whom everyone contemplates, but never becomes a possession owned by anyone, even by his disciples.

Present-day believers, like those of the first century, will add that as far as they are concerned they are the 'possession owned' by the risen Christ, and draw from this the strength by which they live. Nothing is finer or more true than this, but nothing is more difficult in a world which is less and less religious. Believers of the present day must learn to be subject to Jesus of Nazareth without trying to corner him for themselves, to be the mouth and hands of the risen Christ without claiming a monopoly over the prophet of Nazareth, to make him and his message known, without taking possession of the fruits of this effort, to follow the Master without hoping that their behaviour will be understood as they would wish, and without putting themselves in the position of the Pharisee in the parable (Luke 18.9–14).

The present study will have achieved its aim if it helps some amongst them to understand better that, however united one may be with Christ, one never has a hold on Jesus; and if it persuades some unbelievers that Jesus, the great man, is equally accessible to all men.

NOTES

Chapter 1

1. ET 'Concerning the Intention of Jesus and His Teaching', in Charles H. Talbert (ed.), *Reimarus: Fragments*, SCM Press 1971, pp. 59–270.

2. ET *The Life of Jesus Critically Examined*, reissued SCM Press 1972.

3. ET *The Life of Jesus*, 1864; reissued Everymans Library, n.d.

4. 1906. ET *The Quest of the Historical Jesus*, A. and C. Black 1910.

5. Hutchinson 1965.

6. *Das Messianitäts-und Leidensgeheimnis. Eine Skizze des Lebens Jesu*, 1901; ET *The Mystery of the Kingdom of God.The Secret of Jesus' Messiahship and Passion*, A. and C. Black 1925.

7. *Jésus et la révolution non-violente*, Geneva 1961.

8. *ΙΗΣΟΥΣ ΒΑΣΙΛΕΥΣ ΟΥ ΒΑΣΙΛΕΥΣΑΣ*, Heidelberg 1928–30.

9. *The Death of Jesus*, Gollancz 1963.

10. *Jesus and the Zealots*, Manchester University Press 1967.

11. *Jesus and the Revolutionaries*, Harper and Row, New York 1971.

12. *Jesu, Gestalt and Geschichte* ('The Figure and History of Jesus'), Bern 1957; *Die Botschaft Jesu* ('The Message of Jesus'), Bern 1959.

13. *The Setting of the Sermon on the Mount*, Cambridge University Press 1964.

14. ³1962. ET *Jerusalem in the Time of Jesus*, SCM Press 1969.

15. ('Jesus: The Hidden Years'), Paris 1960.

16. 1945. ET *Jesus in his Time*, Eyre and Spottiswoode 1955.

17. *La Date de la Cène*, 1957; ET *The Date of the Last Supper*, Herder 1965.

18. *Les Évangiles de l'Enfance*, 1967; ET *The Infancy Narratives*, Burns and Oates 1968.

19. ('The Framework of the History of Jesus'), Berlin 1919.

20. *The Life and Ministry of Jesus*, Macmillan 1955.

21. *Jesus*, Reinbeck bei Hamburg 1968.

22. 1932, ²1950; ET *The life of Jesus*, Allen and Unwin 1933.

23. *Rediscovering the Teaching of Jesus*, SCM Press 1967.

24. ET *Jesus*, Kegan Paul, Trench and Trubner 1934.

25. *Jesus*, 1938: ET *Jesus*, SCM Press 1963.

26. *The Prophet from Nazareth*, McGraw-Hill, New York 1961.

27. *Jesus, Prophet und Messias aus Galiläa*, Frankfurt am Main 1970.

28. *The Founder of Christianity*, Collins 1971.

29. *Der Staat im Neuen Testament*, ²1961; ET *The State in the New Testament*, SCM Press 1963; *Jesus und die Revolutionären seiner Zeit*, ²1970: ET *Jesus and the Revolutionaries of his Time*, Harper and Row, New York 1971.

30. *Jésus de Nazareth, mythe ou histoire?*, 1925; ET *Jesus the Nazarene – Myth or History?*, Allen and Unwin 1926.

31. *Histoire et mythe à propos de Jésus Christ*, Paris 1938.

32. *La passion du Christ* ('The Passion of Christ'), Paris 1959.

33. *Le Christ et Jésus* ('The Christ and Jesus'), Paris and Brussels 1968.

34. *The Sacred Mushroom and the Cross*, Hodder and Stoughton 1970.

35. 1896. ET *The So-Called Historical Jesus and the Historic, Biblical Christ*, Fortress Press, Philadelphia 1964.

36. ET *Jesus and the Word*, Fontana Books ²1958.

37. SCM Press.

38. 1956. ET *Jesus of Nazareth*, Hodder and Stoughton 1960.

39. *Jesus. Der Mann aus Nazareth und seine Zeit* ('Jesus. The Man from Nazareth and his Time'), Stuttgart 1969.

40. ('The Kerygma and the Earthly Jesus'), Göttingen 1970.

41. ('History of Jesus'), Paris 1961.

42. 1963. ET *The Gospels and the Jesus of History*, Collins 1968.

43. ('From the Christ of History to the Jesus of the Gospels'), Paris 1969.

44. ET *The Theology of St Luke*, Faber 1960.

Chapter 2

1. A discussion of hypotheses questioning the priority of Mark up to 1963 is given in my *La Formation de l'Évangile selon Marc* ('The formation of the Gospel according to Mark'), Paris 1963, pp. 7–23.

2. For comment on R. L. Lindsey, 'A Modified Two Document Theory of the Synoptic . . . Interdependence', *Novum Testamentum* VI, 1963, pp. 239–63 and W. R. Farmer, *The Synoptic Problem*, Macmillan, New York 1964, see the French original of this book, *Jésus de Nazareth vu par les témoins de sa vie*, Neuchâtel 1972, pp. 23f.

3. ('Synoptic Tradition in the Apostolic Fathers'), Berlin 1957.

4. Supplement to *Novum Testamentum XVII*, Leiden 1967.

5. Cf. C. H. Dodd, *Historical Tradition in the Fourth Gospel*, Cambridge University Press 1963.

6. See *La Formation de l'Évangile selon Marc*, passim.

7. See, for example, Marcel Jousse, *Le Style oral rythmique et mnémotechnique chez les verbo-moteurs* ('Rhythmic and Mnemonic Oral Style among the Agents of Verbal Tradition'), Paris 1925.

8. *The Gospel Tradition and its Beginnings*, Mowbrays 1957.

9. H. Ristow and K. Matthiae (eds.), *Der historische Jesus und der kerygmatische Christus. Beiträge zum Christusverständnis* ('The His-

toric Jesus and the Christ of the Kerygma. Contributions to the Understanding of Christ'), Berlin 1960.

10. 'Die vorösterliche Anfänge der Logientradition. Versuch eines formgeschichtlichen Zugangs zum Leben Jesu', op,. cit., pp. 342–70.

11. ('Jesus at the Origins of Tradition. Materials for Gospel History'), Tournai 1968.

12. *New Testament Theology*, Vol. I, *The Proclamation of Jesus*, SCM Press ²1972.

Chapter 3

1. *Die Geschichte der synoptischen Tradition*, Göttingen ⁴1958. ET, Basil Blackwell ²1968, pp. 69ff.

2. P. Vielhauer, 'Gottesreich and Menschensohn in der Verkündigung Jesu' ('Kingdom of God and Son of Man in the Proclamation of Jesus', 1959) and 'Jesus und der Menschensohn' ('Jesus and the Son of Man', 1963), in: *Aufsätze zum Neuen Testament* (Collected Articles), Munich 1965.

3. Victor Hasler, *Amen*, Zurich 1969.

4. E.g. *The Teaching of Jesus*, Cambridge University Press 1935, esp. pp. 211–34 of the 1963 reprint.

Chapter 4

1. ET Basil Blackwell ²1968, pp. 27–39.

2. Op. cit., pp. 12–27.

3. *Jesus aux origines de la tradition*, Tournai 1968, pp. 142f.

Chapter 5

1. *Historical Tradition in the Fourth Gospel*, Cambridge University Press 1963, pp. 302ff., 325ff., 389f.

2. Oscar Cullmann, *Die Christologie des Neuen Testaments*, 1957. ET *The Christology of the New Testament*, SCM Press ²1963, pp. 278f.

3. *Die Abendmahlsworte Jesu*, ³1960. ET *The Eucharistic Words of Jesus*, SCM Press ²1966, pp. 89–105.

4. E.g. *The Gospel according to St Mark*, Macmillan 1952, pp. 653–64.

5. *The History of the Synoptic Tradition*, Basil Blackwell ²1968, pp. 275–84.

6. Op. cit., p. 270.

7. *The Primitive Christian Calendar*, Vol. I, Cambridge University Press 1952, pp. 75–89, 204–27.

8. G. Schille, 'Das Leiden des Herrn', *Zeitschrift für Theologie und Kirche* 52, 1955, pp. 161–205.

9. E.g. Jean Héring, *Le Royaume de Dieu et sa venue* ('The Kingdom of God and its Coming'), Neuchâtel and Paris ²1959, pp. 111ff.

Chapter 6

1. *The History of the Synoptic Tradition*, Basil Blackwell ²1968, pp. 170–9.
2. *Die Gleichnisreden Jesu* ('The Parables of Jesus'), Tübigen ⁵1910.
3. Nisbet 1935.
4. ⁶1962. ET *The Parables of Jesus*, SCM Press ²1963.

Chapter 7

1. *The Miracles of Jesus*, Leiden 1964.
2. E.g. A. M. Farrer, *A Study in St Mark*, Dacre Press 1951.
3. 'Matthew as Interpreter of the Miracle Stories', in G. Bornkamm, G. Barth and H. J. Held, *Tradition and Interpretation in Matthew*, SCM Press 1963.
4. *Historical Tradition in the Fourth Gospel*, Cambridge University Press 1963, pp. 174ff.
5. *The History of the Synoptic Tradition*, Basil Blackwell ²1968, pp. 231–44.
6. Cf. e.g. M. Smith, 'Prolegomena to a Discussion of Aretalogies, Divine Men, the Gospels and Jesus', *Journal of Biblical Literature* XC, 1971, pp. 174–99.
7. Dodd, op. cit., pp. 6ff., 174ff.
8. Bultmann, op. cit., pp. 239ff.
9. Bultmann, op. cit., pp. 231ff.
10. Bultmann, op. cit., p. 228.
11. ('Miracles and the Gospel: The Personal Thought of the Evangelist Mark'), Paris 1966.
12. E.g. Norman Perrin, *Rediscovering the Teaching of Jesus*, SCM Press 1967; Joachim Jeremias, *New Testament Theology*, Vol. I, SCM Press ²1972.

Chapter 8

1. Cf. D. Flusser, *Jesus*, Reinbeck bei Hamburg 1968, p. 106.
2. Cf. the somewhat negative conclusions of M. Goguel, *The Life of Jesus*, Allen and Unwin 1933, pp. 412ff.
3. Etienne Trocmé, 'L'expulsion des marchands du Temple', *New Testament Studies* 15, 1968–69, pp. 1–22.
4. *ΙΗΣΟΥΣ ΒΑΣΙΛΕΥΣ ΟΥ ΒΑΣΙΛΕΥΣΑΣ*, Heidelberg 1928–30
5. *Jesus and the Zealots*, Manchester University Press 1967, pp. 331ff.
6. M. Hengel, *Die Zeloten*, Leiden 1961.
7. *Le Royaume de Dieu et sa venue*, Neuchâtel ²1959, pp. 111–43.

Chapter 9

1. Cf. the recent book by J. Galot, *La Conscience de Jesus* ('The Consciousness of Jesus'), Gembloux 1971.

INDEX OF NEW TESTAMENT REFERENCES

133